P9-DXR-635

SELECTING
AND CARING
FOR YOUR
DOG

About the Author: Sheldon Rubin, DVM, is a practicing veterinarian in Chicago, IL. He received his Doctorate of Veterinary Medicine from the University of Illinois in 1968. Dr. Rubin has served as President and as Secretary of the Chicago Veterinary Medical Association and is also a member of several state and national associations dealing with the practice of veterinary medicine.

Neither the author nor the Editors of Better Way Books take responsibility for any possible consequences from any treatment or action taken by any person reading or following the information in this book. This book is not intended to replace the professional care of a veterinarian for an animal that is sick or injured. It is designed to help you care for your animal and recognize when professional care is necessary. The author and publisher also advise you to check with a veterinarian before administering any medication or health care preparation to your animal.

Copyright © 1985 by Publications International. Ltd. All rights reserved. This book may not be reproduced or quoted in whole or in part by mimeograph or any other printed means or for presentation on radio, television, videotape or film without written permission from Louis Weber, President

Illustrations: Teri J. McDermott, M.A., Medical Illustrator
Cover Design: Jeff Hapner
Cover Photo: Cindy Cassidy

ISBN: 0-88176-301-2

Printed in Canada

Contents

HOME AND EMERGENCY CARE 102

INTRODUCTION

Dogs and people have been friends for centuries—from the time when humans learned to value the dog's skills as hunter and guardian, to the present day when the companionship of a dog is recognized as a source of deep pleasure and satisfaction to millions of people.

Some dogs still perform the tasks of their ancestors: guarding property, herding cattle, hunting game. Some work for their living as police or guide dogs. But today your wish to own a dog is more likely to spring from an appreciation of the generous companionship a dog can give. So deep, in fact, is the friendship that can exist between a person and a pet that scientists have given it a name—they call it the human/companion animal bond, and say that owning a pet helps you feel good, get along with other people—even live longer.

What makes the dog such a good friend? He's loyal, social, demonstrative, and he'll go out of his way to please you. And he doesn't even ask a lot in return—except, of course, your love and loyalty in exchange for his. What else does your dog ask of you? Food and shelter, certainly. Regular grooming and exercise. Routine health care. Medical care if it's necessary.

This book tells how to be your dog's best friend. It's a friendly handbook that discusses everything from choosing the dog that will be happy in your household, to feeding, grooming, and training your dog, to getting along with the veterinarian and knowing what to do in an emergency. So now you can knowledgably be part of the centuries-old tradition of friendship that exists between human beings and dogs.

CHOOSING YOUR DOG: FINDING A FRIEND

No one knows just when the friendship between human beings and dogs first began to develop, but the dog's place in the family certainly dates back to prehistoric times. As far back as known history goes, people and dogs have worked together. So it's a tradition many centuries old that you're perpetuating when you decide to own a dog.

The dog you own today probably won't look much like the dogs known to prehistoric man, and certainly you'll have a far greater variety of different types of dogs to choose from. Selective breeding over the centuries has produced breeds particularly well suited to certain tasks. And the process of natural selection has produced types particularly well suited to different climates and environments.

It's likely, though, that even though your twentieth century dog looks a lot different from his prehistoric ancestors, he'll perform for you some of the same services that early canines performed for your ancestors long ago—keeping you company, helping protect your property, even amusing your children.

The original relationship between dogs and human beings was a working relationship. Dogs herded sheep and cattle, pulled sleds or carts, protected people and their food supply against predators, and retrieved the game shot by hunters. Working dogs still sometimes perform these tasks, but these days it's more likely that you'll want a dog for companionship than for a specific working assignment.

PEOPLE AND DOGS: A SOCIAL RELATIONSHIP

Anyone who has owned a dog knows that a dog is a good and loyal friend. And the dog is a social animal. He adjusts easily to your lifestyle; nothing pleases him more than to please you. He'll take part enthusiastically in your life and that of your family and ask nothing in return except your care and affection. In times of stress the uncritical friendship of a dog can help defuse the tension and calm you down. In fact, after generations of taking the complex human/animal relationship for granted, scientists are now studying the beneficial effects of pet ownership.

As a result of scientific research, there is now medical evidence to prove that the friendly company of a dog can do some people more good than sophisticated medications. Scientists have discovered that Americans who own a pet live longer than those who don't, and that in the act of petting a dog a person's blood pressure drops. Elderly people in nursing homes who seem to have lost the will to live can be brought out of their shells by having a cat or dog to touch and relate to. Children with learning disabilities or behavioral problems often improve dramatically when a pet comes into their lives. In fact, children and older people benefit to such a degree from owning a pet that cats and dogs are now regularly used in therapy by psychologists and psychiatrists. And some withdrawn or disturbed people can learn to respond to animals in preparation for learning to respond to other people.

How do animals help their owners to live longer, feel better, and get along with their neighbors? According to scientists:

• A pet is good company and decreases the owner's sense of loneliness or isolation;

• Taking care of a pet keeps the owner busy;

• Being responsible for an animal's well-being increases the owner's motivation and interest in things outside him or herself;

• A pet can be touched, petted, and handled, thus satisfying a person's emotional need to be in physical contact with another living creature.

Veterinarians will point out that they've known all along that pet ownership is good for people. They'll admit, however, that professionals concerned with the health of both the animal and the human species are excited by new developments in the area the scientists describe as the Human/companion animal bond.

Fortunately for you, your dog will instinctively follow the example of his ancestors as your protector—and, after companionship, protection is the most common reason that people acquire a dog. A dog has a strong urge to protect his own territory—and for your dog that means you and your home. Even a small dog will bark to warn you of an intruder at the door or on your property. In fact, convicted burglars have said that a small, noisy dog is better protection against intrusion than a large dog that looks ferocious; no criminal likes to have attention drawn to his activities. And a large dog at your side when you're out walking is likely to discourage would-be troublemakers.

UNDERSTANDING YOUR DOG'S PAST

The guarding instinct isn't the only working instinct your dog will demonstrate, and you'll find it interesting to note

that although many working and sporting dogs are no
longer used for the work they were originally called on to do,
they retain their instinct to perform. Your Border collie may
anxiously circle a group of other dogs, or even children,
until he's got them all together in one place; this behavior is a
throwback to the job his ancestors were bred to do—herding
sheep. Some small breeds, like Welsh corgis, have a tendency to snap at the heels of dogs (or people)—it's the way their
ancestors rounded up cattle. Pointers who have never been
used for hunting will stop and "point" when they see or smell
a squirrel or a rabbit. That's how they would alert a hunter
to the location of the prey.

Even if you acquire a mixed-breed dog, you can
often make a good guess at his ancestry by watching the way
he behaves. And many of these behavioral patterns can be
useful clues when you're making a choice about the kind of
dog you'd like to have as a pet.

Even before you decide what kind of dog you want,
however, you ought to take a good look at why you want a
dog at all. Is it for companionship? As a friend for the
children? As a guard dog—formally trained to guard or
simply to provide a good loud warning bark or an impres-
sive presence? Do you want a dog that you can exhibit at
breed shows or obedience trials? Do you plan to breed your
dog?

A LONG-TERM COMMITMENT

Whichever answer you give, remind yourself that *any* dog
will make certain demands on you—long-term demands, at
that. Any dog, St. Bernard or Pekingese, purebred or mutt,
will cost you time, energy, and money. All dogs need food,
shelter, and routine medical care—vaccinations, for instance.
They get sick and sometimes need specialized care that can
be expensive. You'll need leashes and grooming equipment.
If you travel, you have to take the dog along or make special
arrangements to have him cared for. Moreover, your dog
has to be socially acceptable; it's up to you to train him to do
as he's told and not be a nuisance to others. This isn't just a

courtesy to your neighbors, either—it's illegal to allow a dog to be a nuisance to other people. By law, you must license your dog and get him vaccinated against rabies.

And owning a dog is a long-term commitment. A healthy dog may well live 15 years or more. So that bounding puppy playing with the kids will still be around when the kids are off on their own. And he'll still be your responsbility.

WHAT KIND OF DOG IS RIGHT FOR YOU?

So do you *really* want a dog? If you've taken a good look at the long-term responsibilities of dog ownership and decided that you're willing and able to take them on, it's time to make the next decision: What kind of a dog is going to fit into your life most satisfactorily. Answer the following questions to help yourself make a decision:

How Will the Dog Fit—Literally— into Your Home?

In other words, what size dog do you want? Very often, circumstances outside your control will answer this question for you. Large dogs take up a lot of space and usually need a lot of exercise (although some small breeds are very lively). If you're living in a small apartment you can't accommodate that cute puppy when you know that by this time next year he's going to be the size of the sofa. So forget about the St. Bernards and German shepherds and turn your attention to something that's more practical in size—like a toy breed or a terrier.

Who's Going to Exercise the Dog?

As mentioned earlier, most large breeds need regular exercise and lots of it, and some small breeds are a lot more energetic than you might expect. Beagles, for instance, have great stamina and need plenty of exercise. Otherwise, they'll bounce around indoors and drive you crazy. And where will the dog urinate and defecate? Remember that in some areas you're legally responsible for cleaning up after him. Will you have to exercise the dog yourself, or can you recruit family members to do some of it? Do you have a big yard where the dog can play, or must you walk him on a leash to the nearest park every time he needs to run? If your space and/or your energy is at a premium, choose a dog that's a natural stay-at-home, not an outdoorsy type.

How Much Dog Can You Feed?

All dogs cost money—no matter their size. Routine vaccinations, checkups, licenses, and, in some cases, boarding kennel fees and special grooming needs, are inevitable expenses for any dog owner. But it's clearly true that a miniature schnauzer eats less than a German shepherd, so if your budget is tight do yourself a favor and don't get a dog that's going to eat as much as a small horse.

What About Temperament?

Dogs, like people, have different personalities: some are lively, some are lazy; some are high-strung, some aren't ruffled by anything. Decide what sort of dog will be temperamentally suitable for your household. And don't imagine that if you want a "quiet" dog you've got to pick a small one. Some large breeds, like Labrador retrievers, are usually extremely easygoing and even-tempered. The chart at the end of this chapter lists the characteristic traits of popular breeds of dogs and can help you judge if a certain type is going to be temperamentally suited to you and your family. Which brings you to the next point:

Does the Dog Like Children?

How well a dog gets along with children depends on several issues: heredity, training, past experience, and so on. If you want a dog that's good with kids you won't choose one that's traditionally short-tempered or snappy—a Chihuahua, for instance. Nor will you choose one that's too timid to be able to cope with boisterous children. If you're getting your pet from a humane shelter, you'll need to check out his temperament carefully. A dog that's been abused or mishandled in the past is less likely to fit in with children than a healthy puppy who has learned to trust humans from his earliest days.

How Much Work Will He Be?

An important consideration is how much care a dog needs beyond the obvious considerations like routine grooming and veterinary checkups. Long-haired dogs clearly require more grooming than short-haired dogs; some, like Afghan hounds and Old English sheepdogs, must be groomed every day. Are you willing to do it? And, even if you're willing, do you have the time? If you're on a tight schedule and know you wouldn't have time to exercise a lively young Doberman pinscher, you wouldn't have time to untangle the shaggy coat of an Old English sheepdog, either. As you see, practical considerations inevitably put some limits on your choices. And there's another aspect of your dog's looks that you have to consider—will maintaining your dog's coat be an added expense? Some breeds require periodical professional grooming and trimming. Do you want to make the regular trips to the canine beauty shop? And are you willing to pick up the bill?

      Grooming isn't the only factor to consider when you're deciding whether or not to have a long-haired dog. There's also the question of shedding. Some long-haired breeds—one is the Norwegian elkhound—have a dense undercoat which traps dead hair. If the dog is not groomed properly he'll shed for longer periods than is normal. So you'll wind up grooming the rugs and furniture as well as the dog.

You must also consider whether anyone in your family is allergic to dog dander (the dried flakes of skin that come away when the animal sheds). If so, you'd be better off with a dog that sheds less and is less likely to trigger allergic reactions. Poodles, schnauzers, and Maltese terriers are among breeds that shed little and are well suited to mildly allergic people.

HOW MUCH DO YOU TRAVEL?

Your lifestyle and the amount of traveling you do also affect your choice of a dog. If you're a homebody and your annual two weeks with your aunt (who lives in the next state and loves dogs anyway) is the extent of your traveling, you probably won't worry too much about boarding kennels and travel restrictions. If you're always on the move, however, you've got to consider what you'll do with your dog while you're away. It's easier to pack a dachshund than a Great Dane. You can more easily ask a friend to come in and care for a small dog than one that's used to daily five mile hikes. And, if you have to board your dog, the rates for a small dog will be lower than for a giant.

THREE NITTY GRITTY QUESTIONS

Now you've got a good idea of the *kind* of dog that will fit—for practical, financial, and temperamental purposes— into your household. There are still three nitty-gritty questions to answer:

• Do you want a male or female dog?

• Do you want a purebred or a mutt?

• Do you want a puppy or an adult?

Take them one by one. Each is an either/or question, and in the last two there are specific advantages and disadvantages to each alternative.

The sex of the dog you want to buy is largely a matter of choice. Neither sex is healthier than the other. Female dogs are somewhat calmer and less excitable than males, but unless you have your female dog spayed you'll have to keep her confined or well under control during her two yearly fertile or heat periods, which last about three weeks each. Male dogs tend to be more aggressive than females, they tend to roam more, and they sometimes have socially unacceptable habits like trying to "mount" people or marking their territory by urinating on the furniture. Neutering the male dog usually causes these undesirable characteristics to subside.

If you want a dog that you can exhibit in breed (or conformation) shows or obedience trials, then obviously you're looking for a purebred. The actual process of choosing one will be discussed later. Purebred dogs are more expensive than mixed breeds—they can be *very* expensive. The rarer the breed the more expensive it becomes, so if you want the prestige of owning a dog that's a class act you'll have to pay for it.

Don't, however, make the mistake of buying a dog just because it's unusual. Find out all you can about the breed first. This is not hard to do, because years and years of selective breeding have given dog fanciers a good idea of what to expect from a certain breed in terms of appearance, character, health considerations, and longevity. But there's a catch: indiscriminate or inbreeding has produced dogs that are not representative of the breed, or that have a marked tendency to hereditary defects. It's essential, therefore, to buy a purebred only from a reputable kennel, and to know what you're looking for before you buy.

Apart from status, however, there's no difference between a dog with a pedigree and dog that's a mixture of all sorts of breeds. You may find, in fact, that a mutt has inherited the best of all its ancestors.

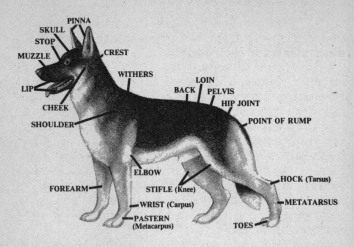

Do you want a puppy or an adult dog? This can be an emotional decision. Puppies are cute. *All* puppies are cute. If you have kids, they'll probably beg you to get a cute puppy. Remember, though, that you're not buying the dog just for the children. As mentioned earlier, the dog will probably still be around when the children are long gone. And it's always a mistake to succumb and get a puppy for a child who absolutely promises to take care of it all by him or herself. Trying to make a child take on full responsibility for a pet never works. It's unfair to everyone—the child, the dog, and you. When you're tempted, remember the huge numbers of dogs that are put to sleep each year in humane shelters, or that wander the streets without a home. A lot of them started out as puppies some youngster promised to take care of all by himself. Don't take any chances that the cute puppy your kids talk you into buying will turn into a big dog you can't cope with, and will sooner or later wind up among the pathetic army of dogs nobody wants.

Puppies demand a great deal of time, attention, and patience, but there are advantages to getting a dog as a puppy. A puppy who's had no previous experience of living with people will adjust more easily to the routine of your household than an adult dog. He'll know who's boss right from the start. You'll be able to train him yourself, and you won't have to correct any ingrained bad habits. And a puppy that you've loved and cared for from the beginning is likely to grow into a contented, good-tempered dog.

If you'd rather avoid the bouncy puppy stage and get an older dog, it's a good idea to go to a reputable animal shelter or humane society. There's no shortage of dogs available for adoption, and you'll be giving a home to a dog that might otherwise be destroyed. Although you'll know nothing of the dog's parentage, the shelter should be able to alert you to any behavior problems the dog may have as a result of past mismanagement or abuse—but don't assume all shelter dogs have problems; many have no problems beyond the need for a home.

A grown dog that has been mistreated, however, may require more time and patience from you than even a small puppy. He may also be set in his ways and accustomed to doing things differently from what you expect, and it may be hard work convincing him that you are now in charge. But if you don't want a puppy—or don't mind much either way—and you're willing to take into account the fact that an adult dog may have some socialization problems that you'll have to straighten out, you'll find a good friend in an adult dog.

SELECTING YOUR DOG: THE DO'S AND DON'TS

Lets assume you've decided to get a dog, and you have some idea about the kind of dog you'd like to share your home with. You're ready to buy your dog, but don't rush into it. Here, as elsewhere, impulse buying can get you into a lot of trouble. Where you get the dog from is as important as the sort of dog you get. If you're looking for a purebred dog, go to breed shows and talk to owners. Buy dog magazines and study them, or go to the library and read up on the different breeds. Look on bulletin boards in the grocery stores. Check the advertisements in your local newspapers. Ask around. Call the local veterinarians. Very often a veterinarian will know of dogs that are available for sale or adoption. Visit humane shelters and observe the physical environment (it should be clean and pleasant) and the condition of the animals.

You can acquire a dog from one of several sources, the most common being a private owner, a breeding kennel, or a shelter or humane society. Whichever source you choose, certain basic rules and safeguards apply, and there are signs that can alert you to the fact that the source is less than reputable. You won't go far wrong if you keep in mind the following do's and don'ts:

• *Don't* buy a puppy before it's six weeks old—the ideal age is eight weeks. Puppies that are removed from the litter too soon often develop strong attachments to people but don't get along with other dogs. Conversely, the longer a puppy is deprived of affectionate human contact, the longer he'll take to adjust to people later on.

• *Don't* buy from any establishment that is not clean and orderly, or where the dogs seem listless and out of condition. Unsanitary surroundings breed unhealthy puppies.

• *Don't* buy from a "puppy mill"—a place that seems to be full of puppies of many different breeds.

• *Don't* buy from any owner who won't let you come into the house to inspect the dog, or won't let you spend time alone with the dog.

• *Don't* buy from any owner who seems reluctant to answer your questions or provide a detailed medical history of the dog.

• *Don't* accept a dog from an owner who won't give you an unconditional guarantee that, if your veterinarian finds something wrong with the dog in the first two or three days after purchase, you can return the dog for a full refund of your purchase price.

• *Don't* believe anyone who tells you that a puppy under four months old has had "all his shots." It can't be true.

• And when you're choosing from a litter of puppies, *don't* choose the one that's shivering in a corner—even if you feel sorry for him. He's the "runt," or weakest of the litter, and he may never grow into a really healthy dog.

• *Don't* accept a puppy that has diarrhea; it can be the sign of internal parasites or other health problems.

• *Do* check on the reputation of the establishment you're getting the dog from. Ask your veterinarian or, if you're buying a purebred, check with breed club for that type of dog. (Breed clubs are organizations of people with a special interest in one breed of dog, and they know all the main breeders in the country.) You can find the name and address of the breed club you're interested in from the American Kennel Club (AKC) which was established in 1884 as a non-profit organization devoted to the advancement of purebred dogs. The AKC is made up of over 400 dog clubs throughout the United States. It maintains a registry of recognized breeds and enforces rules and regulations governing all dog shows under the Club's direction. The official magazine of the AKC is *Pure-Bred Dogs–American Kennel Gazette* which contains everything you ever wanted to know regarding pure bred dog information. You can write to American Kennel Club at 51 Madison Avenue, New York, New York, 10010.

     The United Kennel Club (UKC) maintains the second largest registry in the U.S. and registers a number of breeds not recognized by the AKC. The United Kennel Club is located at 100 E. Kilgore Road, Kalamazoo, Michigan, 49001.

• *Do,* if at all possible, observe a puppy's parents and check out their temperaments. Aggressive parents breed aggressive puppies. Although the environment you provide for the puppy will have a lot to do with molding his personality, seeing the parents will give you a 50 percent chance of predicting what to expect as the puppy grows up. If you're buying a purebred puppy, do be aware of any hereditary defects the breed is susceptible to—if you've done your homework, you'll know what they are. Ask the breeder if a veterinarian has checked the puppy for these defects.

• *Do* be impressed by the professional or home breeder who has these checks completed routinely before offering puppies for sale, and who encourages you to have the puppy examined by your veterinarian immediately after purchase. Any reputable breeder will give you the option of returning the dog if your veterinarian finds anything wrong in the early days.

• *Do* make sure, if you're buying a purebred dog, that the breeder gives you the necessary papers. When you buy a purebred dog that comes from AKC registered parents, you should be given an AKC form filled out by the seller. When you complete this form and send in the proper fee, your dog will be registered also. It is the seller's responsibility to provide you with all the necessary registration forms.

The breeder should also give you a copy of your dog's pedigree, or family tree. Note that a pedigree is, in itself, no guarantee that your purebred dog will do well in dog shows. Basically, all the pedigree tells you is that for three generations back the puppy comes from purebred stock.

A good breeder who knows you're buying the dog for show purposes will not, however, sell you a dog that doesn't show promise of becoming a good "show specimen." Breed clubs are closely knit enclaves where everyone knows everyone else, and the breeder's reputation is on the line. So it's clearly in the breeder's best interest to sell only puppies that will do credit to the kennel's name. In fact, sometimes a breeder will sell you a puppy (or an older dog) only on the understanding that it is not up to show standards, and that you will not exhibit it.

• If you're getting the dog for your family, *don't* hesitate to

take the whole family along to see how the dog reacts. If you
have young children, ask the owner how the dog gets along
with children and how he reacts to a lot of excitement.
Puppies usually love to play and bound around with children, but an older dog who has lived a quiet, sedate life
around adults may have a hard time adjusting to a livelier
environment.

• *Do* spend time alone with the dog you plan to buy. Take
the puppy away from his littermates to see how he reacts—a
well adjusted puppy will enjoy the extra attention and fon-
dling; a weak or very shy puppy will probably be undemon-
strative and appear lethargic or overly timid, and maybe
you'll want to choose a more sociable pup. If you're buying
an adult dog, spend a few minutes with him away from his
owner; this will give you a chance to estimate how willing the
dog is to make friends with someone new. If he snarls or
shrinks away from your friendly approach he may have had
bad experiences which will make for a difficult adjustment
period. This opportunity to check each other out is particularly important when you're getting a dog from a shelter,
and have no knowledge of his parentage or past beyond
what the shelter staff can tell you from their own observa-
tions.

• Above all, *do* ask as many questions as you want. A
reputable owner or breeder who's anxious to place an animal
in a good home will be more than glad to answer all your
queries. Any reluctance to answer questions or to let you see
the environment is a sure sign that you'd do better to look
elsewhere.

WELL-BRED DOGS

A brief guide to some of the most popular dogs in the six purebred groups.

SPORTING DOGS

COCKER SPANIEL*   *Ht. 14-15 inches, wt. 22-28 pounds*

Smallest sporting dog. Sturdy. Popular house dog. Affectionate and loyal. Requires grooming.

GERMAN SHORT-HAIRED POINTER   *Ht. 21-25 inches,*
                                           wt. 45-70 pounds

Good hunter. Easy to train. Has tendency to wander. Good family pet. Does best in country rather than city.

GOLDEN RETRIEVER*   *Ht. 20-24 inches, wt. 55-70 pounds*

Good hunter. Very intelligent. Used as guide dog for the blind. Great family dog and excellent with children. Needs exercise.

IRISH SETTER   *Ht. 23-27 inches, wt. 50-70 pounds*

Very popular dog. Good sense of smell. Good hunter. Temperamental and stubborn, but good with children.

LABRADOR RETRIEVER*   *Ht. 21-24 inches, wt. 55-75 pounds*

Very intelligent. Used as guide dog for the blind. Good hunter. Fine family pet and gentle with children. Needs exercise.

SPRINGER SPANIEL   *Ht. 18-20 inches, wt. 45-55 pounds*

Intelligent. Fast. Good bird hunter. Affectionate. Loyal family pet but somewhat stubborn. Needs exercise.

WEIMARANER   *Ht. 23-27 inches, wt. 55-85 pounds*

Intelligent, affectionate animal. Good house dog but not terrific with children. Needs exercise.

One of the 10 most popular breeds in the United States according to the American Kennel Club's 1981 figures.

HOUNDS

AFGHAN HOUND   *Ht. 25-29 inches, wt. 50-60 pounds*

Not reliable around children, but excellent pet for adults. Needs exercise and lots of grooming.

BASSET HOUND   *Ht. 11-15 inches, wt. 50 pounds*

Gentle, devoted animal. Good family pet. Does well in city. Stubborn, so is difficult to train.

BEAGLE*   *Ht. 13-15 inches, wt. 20-30 pounds*

Good indoor and outdoor dog. Great for a family. Barks a lot. Stubborn, so is difficult to train.

DACHSHUND*   *Ht. 9-10 inches, wt. 18-20 pounds*

Better with adults than children. Good house pet. Affectionate. Barks at strangers. Prone to back problems.

IRISH WOLFHOUND   *Ht. 30-34 inches, wt. 100-140 pounds*

Most gentle of all dogs. Affectionate and intelligent. Patient. Great with children. Needs lots of room.

NORWEGIAN ELKHOUND   *Ht. 18-21 inches, wt. 50 pounds*

Friendly. Intelligent. Active family pet. Very loyal. Good with children. Requires regular grooming.

WORKING DOGS

ALASKAN MALAMUTE   *Ht. 22-25 inches, wt. 50-90 pounds*

Great endurance and strength. Despite Arctic heritage, adapts well to all climates. Aggressive with other dogs. Not tolerant of young children. Requires exercise and regular grooming. Barks seldom. Very clean.

BOXER   *Ht. 21-25 inches, wt. 60-80 pounds*

Excellent family pet. Gentle and good with children. Affectionate and playful. Needs plenty of exercise. Smooth, short-haired coat.

---

*One of the 10 most popular breeds in the United States according to the American Kennel Club's 1981 figures.

COLLIE   *Ht. 22-26 inches, wt. 50-75 pounds*

Excellent family pet. Somewhat independent. Great with children. Requires regular grooming.

DOBERMAN PINSCHER*   *Ht. 24-28 inches, wt. 60-75 pounds*

Good watch dog. Excellent family pet. Easy to train with firm discipline. Often is a one owner dog, i.e. loyal to one family member.

GERMAN SHEPHERD*   *Ht. 22-26 inches, wt. 60-85 pounds*

Most popular breed in world. Hardy. Intelligent. Good family pet. Good with children. Used as guide dog for the blind.

GREAT DANE   *Ht. 30 inches or more, wt. 120-150 pounds*

Good family dog. Affectionate. Good with children. Aggressive if threatened. Needs exercise.

NEWFOUNDLAND   *Ht. 28 inches, wt. 150 pounds*

Great family pet. Good with children. One of the sweetest-tempered of the large breeds. Intelligent. Fast learner.

OLD ENGLISH SHEEPDOG   *Ht. 21-25 inches, wt. 75-90 pounds*

Excellent house dog but needs exercise. Requires considerable grooming and sheds heavily in summer.

ST. BERNARD   *Ht. 25-29 inches, wt. 165-175 pounds*

Good family pet and watch dog. Needs early obedience training. Sheds heavily and needs grooming. Good with children.

SHETLAND SHEEPDOG (Sheltie)*   *Ht. 14-16 inches, wt. 16 pounds*

Good in limited space. Obedient. Excellent with children. Demands affection. Needs grooming.

SIBERIAN HUSKY   *Ht. 20-24 inches, wt. 35-60 pounds*

Gentle, friendly, and good with children. Nonaggressive with other dogs. Needs lots of outdoor exercise. Sheds heavily.

One of the 10 most popular breeds in the United States according to the American Kennel Club's 1981 figures.

TERRIERS

AIREDALE   *Ht. 22-24 inches, wt. 40-50 pounds*

Good house dog but independent. Good with children. Needs exercise.

BEDLINGTON TERRIER   *Ht. 16 inches, wt. 17-23 pounds*

Extremely affectionate. Good family dog. Good with children. Sheds little.

CAIRN TERRIER   *Ht. under 10 inches, wt. under 14 pounds*

Very intelligent. Lively disposition. Good family dog with older children. Requires little grooming.

KERRY BLUE TERRIER   *Ht. 18-19 inches, wt. 30-40 pounds*

Intelligent. Alert. Good family dog. Unusually long-lived.

MINIATURE SCHNAUZER*   *Ht. 11-14 inches, wt. 15 pounds*

Strong-willed and independent. Needs exercise. Fairly high strung and not good with small children. Good watch dog. Needs grooming.

SCOTTISH TERRIER (Scottie) *Ht. 10-11 inches, wt. 17-21 pounds*

Great for apartment dwellers. Active. Intelligent. Not reliable around children.

WELSH TERRIER   *Ht. 14-15 inches, wt. 18-21 pounds*

Active house dog. Good watch dog. Good with children. Needs grooming.

WEST HIGHLAND WHITE TERRIER (Westi)   *Ht. 10-11 inches,*
                                             wt. 14-19 pounds

Good family dog. Good with older children. Easy to groom.

One of the 10 most popular breeds in the United States according to the American Kennel Club's 1981 figures.

TOYS

CHIHUAHUA	*Ht. about 5 inches, wt. 1-6 pounds*

Smallest of all dogs. Intelligent. Easy to train. Friendly. Good house dog. Loyal. Good watch dog. Not good with small children.

MALTESE TERRIER	*Ht. 5-7 inches, wt. 2-7 pounds*

Loyal. Intelligent. Excellent house dog. Good watch dog. Good with children. Needs grooming.

PEKINGESE	*Ht. 6-10 inches, wt. 7-10 pounds*

Good, loyal pet. Very companionable. Independent and stubborn. Not recommended for families with children.

POMERANIAN	*Ht. 5-7 inches, wt. 3-7 pounds*

Intelligent. Alert. Good house dog but not good with children.

PUG	*Ht. 10-12 inches, wt. 14-18 pounds*

Very intelligent but very stubborn. Has breathing problems. Does not do well in hot weather. Sheds little. Good with children.

SHIH TZU	*Ht. 9-11 inches, wt. 12-15 pounds*

Independent, but wonderful house dog. Great with children.

YORKSHIRE TERRIER	*Ht. 7-9 inches, wt. 5-8 pounds*

Intelligent, high-spirited, and friendly. Very popular house dog. Good with children. Sheds little.

NON-SPORTING DOGS

BOSTON TERRIER	*Ht. 14-16 inches, wt. 15-25 pounds*

Very good family pet. Somewhat intolerant of young children. Often needs Caesarean section for delivery of pups.

One of the 10 most popular breeds in the United States according to the American Kennel Club's 1981 figures.

BULLDOG *Ht. 14-16 inches, wt. 40-50 pounds*

Wonderful family pet. Excellent with children and strangers. Needs little grooming. Has whelping problems and breathing problems.

CHOW CHOW *Ht. 18-20 inches, wt. 50-60 pounds*

Only dog with blue-black tongue. Very powerful. Devoted family pet. Best with older children. Does not trust strangers.

DALMATIAN *Ht. 19-23 inches, wt. 50-55 pounds*

Very intelligent. Loyal house pet. Needs plenty of exercise. Best with older children.

LHASA APSO *Ht. 10-14 inches, wt. 15-16 pounds*

Beautiful, small dog. Excellent house pet. Very independent. Difficult to train. Not always good with small children.

POODLE* Standard *Ht. over 15 inches, wt. 45-55 pounds*
Miniature *Ht. 10-15 inches, wt. 16 pounds*
Toy *Ht. under 10 inches, wt. 7 pounds*

Intelligent, active, alert animal. One of the most popular dogs in the United States. Easily trained. Some miniatures and toys are too excitable to be suitable for families with young children, but standards are very good with children. Sheds little, but requires a lot of coat care, including clipping.

*One of the 10 most popular breeds in the United States according to the American Kennel Club's 1981 figures.

YOUR DOG BECOMES ONE OF THE FAMILY

You have now made some decisions about your dog; you know if you want a male or female, a purebred or a mutt, a puppy or an adult. You've looked into various sources and decided where to get your dog. Now's the time to do some practical preparation for dog ownership. Here's what you need to do before you bring the newcomer home:

- Brief the family on how to treat the newcomer.

- Arrange a sleeping place for the dog.

- Be prepared to provide appropriate food and water.

- Decide where the dog will urinate and defecate and, if the dog is not already trained, make plans for house-breaking.

- Buy a collar and leash if you're planning to take the dog out of the house right away.

- Check on local licensing requirements and regulations that affect dog owners.

- Locate and introduce yourself to a veterinarian.

The arrival of a new pet is always exciting, especially when there are children in the family, but too much action and emotion will disturb and confuse the dog. Remind everyone that over-excitment will panic the dog, that a puppy tires easily just like a baby, and that a grown dog will need time to adjust to a new environment. If you have children, remind them that you're not going to let them carry the puppy around and display him to all their friends—not at first, anyway. For one thing, an animal is not a toy. For another, a puppy will squirm a lot because he's insecure, and may squirm right out of a child's arms and fall.

Remember, also, that in the dog's eyes children are not dominant family members—*you* are the boss. So let the kids know that they are not to try to discipline or train the puppy in the early days. That's your job.

Where will the dog sleep? The sooner you introduce your new pet to his sleeping quarters the better for him—and for you. If the dog is a puppy, you need a place where you can keep him confined until he is trained to be clean in the house. The ideal situation is a room with a gate—like a child's safety gate—across the doorway. And since the dog's going to be part of the family, this area of confinement should be where there's lots of action; the kitchen is a good place.

Put the dog's bed in the room you've chosen, with a layer of papers nearby for him to use for urinating and defecating. Tell everyone that he's to be allowed only in this one room until he's trained.

Sleeping in a confined space is very comforting and dogs, like people, like to have a place of their own. You can buy a dog bed for the newcomer, but it's not strictly necessary. A box lined with a blanket or some of your old sweaters will work just as well—it won't be as smart, but the dog isn't interested in glamor and an article of your clothing will help him get used to your particular smell. Cut the sides of the box down so that he can get out easily.

Whatever sleeping arrangement you make for the dog, be sure that the bed is warm, easy to get in and out of, and out of drafts. Raise the bed off the floor a bit if drafts are a problem. The first few nights that a puppy spends away from the litter can be traumatic for him, and for you. It helps to tuck a hot water bottle into his bed and to set a ticking clock or a quietly playing radio nearby; these surrogates will take the place of the warmth and sounds of the litter and help him feel less lonely.

If the puppy cries the first few nights, be patient. Don't give in and let him sleep in your bedroom or on your bed; you'd be setting a precedent you may not be happy with later. After a few nights he'll quiet down and be content in his own bed. The same goes for the older dog—although in this case you can dispense with the hot water bottle and the clock.

During the time you're training or house-breaking your puppy, you can keep him confined in a wire cage, or crate, instead of in a single room. These crates are available at any pet supplier and usually are collapsible when not in use. The best type lets the dog see out on all four sides. Basically, the crate is like a baby's playpen, and it should be big enough for the dog to lie down and turn around, but small enough so that if he eliminates in the crate he will be soiling his own bed. The whole idea is that the puppy will not, or should not, relieve himself where he sleeps. If you choose to use a crate remember two things:

• The cage must be large enough to accommodate the dog so that he can turn around and lie down comfortably.

• The puppy must be kept in the crate at all times when you're not home, and must sleep in the crate at night. (The actual process of house-breaking will be discussed later in this section.)

If you want your dog to live outside, you must provide suitable housing to protect him against extremes of heat or cold. When you're buying or building a doghouse or kennel, make sure that it meets the following requirements:

• It must be built above the ground, so that air can circulate underneath the structure and keep the floor dry.

• It must be big enough for the dog to move around in comfortably.

• It must be sheltered from direct sun or strong winds.

• Bedding—hay or wood shavings, for instance—must be changed frequently.

If you're also constructing a dog run—a place where the dog can exercise and also urinate and defecate—your main concerns are safety and sanitation. The run must be escape-proof with sides high enough to deter the dog from jumping out. And it must be easy to clean; gravel is fairly easy to maintain, and concrete flooring is ideal because you can hose it off and disinfect it very easily. Grass or dirt runs cannot be cleaned effectively, and can harbor the eggs of parasites like roundworms and hookworms for an indefinite length of time.

What will the newcomer eat? Feeding and nutrition requirements vary according to the age of the dog, and the charts in the next chapter gives guidelines on nutrition for dogs of varying ages. When you adopt a grown dog, it's easy enough to follow the feeding schedule used by the previous owner. If you want to make changes in that schedule, do it gradually. If your veterinarian, in the course of his initial examination, feels that the dog has been getting an inadequate diet, he or she will make recommendations for a special diet.

Feeding a puppy takes a bit more work. Puppies are usually weaned—introduced to solid food—at four to five weeks old. By six to eight weeks the mother is hardly nursing them at all, and she will encourage this independence by pushing them away when they try to nurse. So when you take an eight-week-old puppy home he should be fully weaned and accustomed to solid food. You must, however, feed him at least three or four times a day, and he needs two to three times the calories that he'll need when he's fully grown. Remember, too, that any dog must have a supply of fresh water readily available at all times.

WHAT ABOUT HOUSE-BREAKING?

Training a dog to urinate and defecate only outdoors or in acceptable places is not difficult provided that everyone concerned with the dog understands the routine and follows it consistently.

If you are training a puppy in a single room or in a crate, place several thicknesses of newspaper in one corner of the room, and put his food and water nearby. A young puppy needs to void urine or feces, or both, immediately after eating, so as soon as he's finished his food pick him up and put him on or near the papers. When he uses the papers, make a big fuss of him and let him know that he's done the right thing. If you catch him in the act of voiding off the papers, pick him up immediately and put him on the papers.

When he gets it right, praise him lavishly. Don't ever discipline if you don't actually see him making a mistake. An animal can't associate punishment with a past act. And be very careful how you discipline when you're trying to house-break a dog. Physical punishment is not necessary; a stern voice is all you need. If you're too rough you'll end up with a dog that's scared all the time.

When the puppy is using the paper 100 percent of the time, he is ready to venture out of the confinement area. But even now watch every move until you're quite sure he's not going to transfer his attention from the training papers to a corner of your best rug.

If you choose not to paper train, be prepared to spend a good deal of time taking the puppy outside. Immediately when he wakes from sleeping, take him out to the area you've designated for his use and set him down. If he voids, praise him and make a big fuss about how clever he is. If you take him out to the same place every two hours he should soon get the idea of what you want him to do.

If you're outdoor training a puppy and keeping him in a cage between outings, don't be disturbed if he voids in the cage. You've probably heard that a dog will never soil his sleeping quarters, and this usually holds true for older dogs.

But a young puppy can't hold his urine all night and if he's confined in a cage he has no choice but to void right where he is.

Apart from when he wakes up and after eating, there's another time when a puppy may need to urinate and that's after he's been playing hard. Be aware of this and take him to his paper or outdoor spot as soon as the game is over.

Remember that your puppy is a social creature and wants to please you. So with patience, perserverance, and consistency on your part and the part of family members, house-breaking should be a fairly painless procedure for all involved regardless what method you use.

When you bring an older dog into your home you'll need to approach training in a different way. Since the dog is used to other routines, paper training may be a difficult job—especially if the dog has never been trained at all. As with a puppy, you can try paper training or regular trips to the outside area designated for the dog's use. And, as with a younger dog, take the dog outside every two hours and praise him lavishly when he performs in the right place. If the older dog urinates or defecates in the house, scold him *only* when you catch him in the act. Don't rub his nose in any mess he makes; this may relieve your feelings of anger or frustration, but the dog learns nothing from it. Training your older dog may take as long, or even longer, than training a puppy, but the dog will eventually respond to your verbal encouragement and praise. Once he's trained, you'll only need to take him out two or three times a day.

One of your responsibilities as a dog owner is to clean up after your dog. In some areas you're legally required to do so. But even where no specific legal restrictions exist, common sense tells you that the health of your dog depends on the cleanliness of his surroundings. Parasites and germs are transferred in the feces, and if waste is not removed regularly the dog will reinfect himself and infect other dogs.

If your dog uses your back yard or a dog run for voiding, try training him to use an area of concrete or some other hard surface rather than a grassy or overgrown area that cannot easily be washed down. Remove the feces immediately and get rid of them. The same applies if your dog voids off your property. It's your responsibility to remove the feces and dispose of them. This is particularly important in urban areas where there are heavy concentrations of dogs many of which are, unfortunately, allowed to run loose. Constant soiling of the ground in such areas makes for a year-round parasite problem.

There are a number of commercial "pooper-scoopers" on the market that you can use to remove your dog's feces. Some of these have long handles so you don't have to bend. Or you can use a small shovel and a plastic bag—it's just as effective. If every dog owner regularly cleaned up after his pet, the streets would be healthier and more pleasant for everyone, and there would be less hostility between people who own dogs and people who don't.

WHAT ABOUT LEASHES AND GROOMING AIDS?

The type of basic grooming equipment you need—there's not much of it, in any case—depends on the type of dog you have. And you don't always have to buy it before you get the dog. Sooner or later, however, you will need these items:

Collar and leash.   In many areas, particularly urban areas, you are legally required to keep your dog on a leash. If you have a larger dog, you will also need a chain choke collar. This is, as the name suggests, a chain that can be loosened or tightened as required. It's a valuable aid when you're obedience training a dog, and will restrain a large dog from taking *you* for a walk, rather than the other way around. The chain forms a collar, and if the dog lunges, the chain tightens automatically and restrains him. Always use a chain choke with care—if you're careless you can, literally, choke the dog; at the least you can make him very uncomfortable and cause him to cough. Let your veterinarian demonstrate how to use the chain and where it should, and should not, lie on the dog's neck. Buy a chain choke collar that is one inch longer than the measurement round the largest part of your dog's neck.

Nail clippers. Unless a dog exercises enough on hard ground to keep his nails worn down, you will have to clip them. Use only clippers intended for dogs, not those intended for people. Your veterinarian will recommend a brand, and detailed instructions for clipping a dog's nails are given in the chapter on grooming.

Brush and comb. The length of the dog's coat determines the type of brush and comb you'll use. Refer to the section on grooming and the illustrations there to decide what's best for your dog.

THE LEGALITIES OF OWNING A DOG

Besides being a good neighbor and doing everything possible to prevent your neighbor from disliking your dog, you are obligated by certain laws to carry out certain tasks. Most communities have leash laws which require your dog never to be off leash when outside your property. Many areas require you to clean up your dog's feces, and in certain cities dogs must eliminate only in the curb of the street. These "scooper" laws are designed to eliminate dog feces from public and private grounds in order to control the transmission of disease and prevent dogs from getting a reputation as a nuisance. Rabies vaccinations are required by law in every state of the United States, and most areas also require that you license your dog. The cost of the license frequently helps support the local animal pound.

Unfortunately, all these laws were made necessary because irresponsible owners allowed their dogs to run loose and harass farm animals, wildlife, and people, and to soil lawns, gardens, and public parks. In fact, being a responsible pet owner requires very little effort beyond normal consideration for other people. You can call your local city hall or municipal building for information on requirements in your area.

You, Your Dog, and the Veterinarian

As soon as you acquire a dog, you should have him checked out by a veterinarian. And if you've never owned a dog before, how do you locate a good veterinarian? First, ask your pet-owning friends—they're probably as familiar with their veterinarian as with their physician and chose him or her for the same reasons: professional competence, reasonable fees, convenience of hours and location, and genuine interest in his or her patients. If none of your friends are pet owners, call up the local veterinary association and ask for recommendations.

Once you've decided on a veterinarian, call up, introduce yourself, and arrange to visit the facility. Veterinarians, like doctors, are often very busy, but they are always happy to show you around.

What are you looking for in this initial visit to the veterinarian? Basically, you're checking out these points:

• Is the facility clean, orderly, and pleasant? A veterinarian's office should be as clean as your own doctor's.

• Is emergency service available? If your dog gets sick or is involved in an accident out of office hours, what will you do? Many veterinarians belong to emergency clinics which function after their own hospital closes. Be sure that your veterinarian is a member of such a clinic, or has some other adequate emergency service available.

• Is the veterinarian willing to answer all your questions? A good veterinarian will be able to answer your questions in understandable terms—you and the veterinarian, after all, are partners in caring for your pet's health. Your veterinarian should also explain the fee scale for different services.

• Are the two of you going to get along on a professional level? It's important that you feel comfortable with the person who'll be caring for your pet. Lack of communication is one of the most common reasons that client and veterinarian part company.

Communication between client and veterinarian works both ways. Treat the veterinarian as you would your own doctor. Don't make unnecessary calls. Follow the veterinarian's instructions precisely. And, as you become a more experienced dog owner, use your judgment to decide what is an emergency and what isn't.

Your dog's first visit to the veterinarian's office should be within a few days of the new pet's arrival in your home.

At this first visit your veterinarian will give the dog a thorough physical examination, and, if the dog is a puppy, administer the first of the series of vaccinations that are necessary to protect the animal against a number of canine diseases. At this time the veterinarian will also advise on diet, and set up a future vaccination schedule for the dog. Further information on vaccinations is given in a later chapter. If your dog is a puppy, this first visit to the veterinarian should take place between the ages of six and eight weeks.

Remember to take a sample of the dog's stool along to the veterinarian's office. The stool will be analyzed for parasites and, if necessary, a worming schedule will be set up.

ELECTIVE SURGERY

Your initial visit to the veterinarian with your new pet is an appropriate time to discuss whether or not to have the dog neutered. Apart from the obvious advantage of avoiding accidental parenthood, both male and female animals can benefit from neutering. The procedure reduces the incidence of certain health problems, and contrary to what you may have heard neutering does not have adverse effects on the personality.

Neutering comes under the heading of "elective surgery"—literally, surgery that you choose to have done even though it is not necessitated by any direct health problem.

Neutering, or castrating, the male dog involves the surgical removal of both testes from the scrotum. It is a simple procedure and presents few problems. It's done in the veterinary hospital under general anesthetic and the dog can usually go home the next day. Most veterinarians advise that the male dog should be neutered at the age of one year, although it is possible to neuter a healthy dog at any age.

Male dogs that are not neutered sometimes have a tendency to roam, and may develop socially unacceptable habits such as "mounting" objects or people (that is, assuming the posture for mating), urinating on the furniture, or being very aggressive toward other male dogs. Neutering usually reduces or eliminates these bad habits.

It's not true that neutered dogs become fat, lazy, and unresponsive. Dogs get fat and lazy because they're over-fed and under-excercised, and an unresponsive dog is usually indicating that his owner is not giving him much incentive to respond.

The female dog's reproductive cycle—also known as the estrous or heat cycle—usually begins when she's about eight months old when she comes into heat for the first time. (Note that giant breeds tend to come into heat later. The cycle should begin before the dog is a year old, but sometimes doesn't start until 15 months.) There are exceptions, but most bitches come into heat every six months. The normal heat or estrous cycle lasts about three weeks, and only in the second week is the bitch capable of conceiving.

The first sign that the bitch is in heat is a swelling of the external genitalia (vulva), accompanied by slight bleeding from the vulva. If your dog leads an active social life, you'll notice that every male dog in the neighborhood is suddenly showing up to visit. In fact, since most bitches are very fastidious about cleaning themselves when they're in heat, you may realize that your dog suddenly is surrounded by suitors before you notice the physical signs.

If you plan to breed the bitch, it's advisable to wait

until the second heat because it gives the bitch the chance to mature fully before having puppies. If you do not plan to breed her, it makes sense to have her spayed.

A female dog is made incapable of breeding by a surgical procedure called ovariohysterectomy, more commonly known as spaying. This involves the removal of the ovaries and the uterus; the female's heat periods stop and she cannot, of course, have puppies.

Ideally, the female dog should be spayed at about six months of age, when the procedure is simpler and recovery faster, although spaying can be done at any age with no lasting ill effects. Spaying while she's young significantly reduces the risk of breast cancer and prevents infection of the uterus (pyometra) and false pregnancy.

Spaying does alter the metabolism of the female dog to some extent, and she may put on weight unless her diet is controlled and she gets plenty of excercise. Avoiding weight gain, however, is a simple matter, and spaying may even increase her life span.

Spaying is done under a general anesthetic. An incision is made in the abdomen, the ovaries and utcrus removed, and the incision closed with stitches. The dog must be kept quiet for three to four days, and the stitches can usually be removed after ten days.

Certain purebred dogs that are to be exhibited in dog shows must have their tails docked and/or their dewclaws removed in order to conform to breed standards set by the American Kennel Club. Unless this is done, they cannot be exhibited in AKC shows. Both procedures are carried out when the puppies are three to five days old, when both the discomfort to the pup and the aftercare necessary are minimal. Tail docking involves surgically cutting the tail at a joint. Among the purebreds required to have docked tails are Doberman pinschers, boxers, schnauzers, and poodles.

The dewclaws are the nails located on the inside of the front paws and occasionally on the rear paws; they are more or less equivalent to human thumbs, but (unlike human thumbs) serve no useful function. The dewclaws are removed at the same time that the tail is docked, and even if the procedure is not required by AKC breed standards it's advisable to have it done—expecially in working and hunting dogs whose dewclaws can catch and tear.

Both tail docking and dewclaw removal can be done when the dog is older, but the procedure is a lot more difficult at a later stage of development.

Some breed are usually exhibited with their ears cut (cropped). Doberman pinschers, for instance, have naturally floppy ears that are frequently cropped to a pointed, upstanding, triangular shape. The same is true of miniature schnauzers and Great Danes. Ear cropping is a procedure that should be discussed with a veterinarian. If it is to be done, it should be done when the dog is eight to 12 weeks old. Many countries, England and Canada among them, do not permit ear trimming, and Doberman pinschers, Great Danes and other breeds are exhibited with their natural ears. The decision to crop ears should be made by the owner with the advice of his or her veterinarian.

SAYING GOODBYE

Hard as it may be to think of—especially when you've just acquired a healthy young dog—one of the services your veterinarian may one day have to perform for you is euthanizing your pet. Dogs age faster than people, and begin to fail much earlier. Often an aging dog will lose a lot of weight, want to sleep all day, or become disoriented. Some older dogs start to urinate and defecate in the house. Old age may also bring loss of sight or hearing. Watching an animal you love become debilitated through age or through chronic disease is one of the saddest parts of owning and caring for him.

How do you make that all too final decision to end the dog's life? When your pet can no longer function as a pet or lead a full, comfortable existence, it's time to make the decision to euthanize him. Although it's hard at the time, the decision to euthanize a dog that's either too old or too sick to go on living contentedly is one you cannot regret.

When the question arises, you should discuss it with all family members, including the children, and then with your veterinarian. In fact, the veterinarian is often the first one to realize the need to put the dog to sleep and to make the suggestion.

Euthanasia is a painless procedure in which a drug is injected into the dog. The drug simply acts first to put the dog to sleep, and then to stop the heart. You may want to be with your dog while it's done, but sometimes it's wiser to let the veterinarian perform the euthanasia alone.

Either way, all members of the family must be aware of what is happening. It's particularly important that children understand that the procedure is the best thing for the dog and that it won't hurt him. If you're straight with them they will be able to handle their grief and get over it. After awhile—and psychologists generally agree that it should not be too soon, so don't rush right out and buy another puppy—you can introduce a new pet into the home. If the children have had the opportunity to work through their feelings about the dog that was put to sleep, they won't regard the new dog as a substitute and the newcomer will have a chance to make friends with the family on his own terms.

NUTRITION: HOW TO KEEP YOUR DOG WELL-FED

If you're around dog owners you may hear them remark that the proverbial "dog's life" is actually a very comfortable life—all a dog has to do is eat, sleep, and play. And if you're a new dog owner you certainly want to feed your dog right. The eating part of your dog's life, in fact, is the easiest part of your job. The commercial dog foods now available are easy to use and nutritionally sound—in fact, the increased life span of today's dog over his ancestors is partly due to balanced commercial products which contain all the fats, carbohydrates, essential amino acids, vitamins, and minerals that a normal, healthy dog needs.

Despite the availability of these foods, some pet owners still indulge a dog with tidbits, leftovers from the family table, and so on. The result? An overweight dog. The rationale behind overfeeding or unsuitable feeding is simple: dogs love to please their owners, and owners love to please their dogs; so what better way to show affection than with food? It's a false assumption, however, because obesity is now a major problem among domestic animals, and obesity is the result of overfeeding or of spoiling the animal with table food instead of spoiling him with love and attention.

What kind of food can you feed your dog? Basically, commercial dog foods come in three forms: dry, semi-moist and canned.

Dry dog foods contain only 10 to 12 percent moisture. All the brands have basically the same content of vitamins, minerals, and essential amino acids, but the protein and fat content may vary. Most contain between 20 and 25 percent protein and about 8 percent fat. Dry foods supply approximately 1300 to 1700 calories per pound of product.

Semi-moist foods usually come in sealed packages and supply about 1200 calories per pound of product. Most brands contain approximately 34 percent moisture, 20 percent protein, and 7 percent fat.

Canned dog foods contain a high percentage of moisture—70 to 80 percent. They usually provide about 600 to 700 calories per one-pound can, and have a protein content of 10 to 12 percent and a fat content of about 6 percent. If you're buying a canned food, check the label to make sure that it's marked as a "complete" diet.

The following nutrition guide gives an approximation of how much food a healthy dog will need at different stages of development. Quantities are given according to body weight. Note that these amounts apply only to healthy dogs living in a normal domestic environment. Working dogs, sick or debilitated dogs, some puppies, and pregnant bitches all have specific dietary requirements and should be fed according to the recommendations of a veterinarian.

NUTRITION: THE WELL-FED DOG

- An active adult dog needs about 40 calories per day per pound of body weight. For example, if your active adult dog weighs 40 lbs., he needs 40 lbs. x 40 calories = 1600 calories a day. This is equivalent to about $5\frac{1}{2}$ cups of dry food.

• Your 40 lb. house dog, though, needs only about 30 calories per day per pound of weight—40 x 30 = 1200, or 4 cups of dry food.

• If your 40 lb. dog is older or on a diet, he may need only 25 calories per day per pound. 40 x 25 = 1000 calories, or 3$\frac{1}{2}$ cups of dry food.

• A puppy needs about 60 calories per day per pound of body weight, then that need decreases fairly rapidly until one year of age when he needs only about 40 calories per day per pound.

Use the charts on pages 45 and 48 to estimate how many calories your puppy or adult dog needs daily. It's important to remember, however, that dogs (like people) vary in appetite. These guidelines should be adjusted to the needs of the particular dog.

In order to use this chart, you must know the calorie content per cup, package, or can of product you are feeding. This information should be available on the package or from the manufacturer. As a guide:

1 cup of dry food = 300 calories

1 pkg. semi-moist food (6 oz.) = 400 calories

1 can dog food (16 oz.) = 600 calories

When treats are used, food intake should be reduced to make up for the calories these snacks contain.

To use the puppy chart, find your dog's age in the top line and his weight in the left-hand column. The figure where the two intersect gives you the dog's calorie requirements at that age. For instance, at four months old a 20 lb. puppy needs 1220 calories a day.

FEEDING A PUPPY

When you take an eight-week-old puppy home, he should be completely weaned. Weaning (giving solid food) starts

DAILY CALORIE REQUIREMENTS FOR PUPPIES

Weight		Age					
		6 wks.	3 mos.	4 mos.	6 mos.	8 mos.	1 yr.
				Calories Per Day			
2.3 kgs	5 lbs	525	395	305	265	200	175
4.5	10	1050	790	610	530	400	350
9.1	20	2100	1580	1220	1060	800	700
13.6	30		2370	1830	1590	1200	1050
18.2	40			2440	2120	1600	1400
22.7	50			3050	2650	2000	1750

☐ *These figures are based on the results of scientific studies on dog nutrition.*
☐ *Note that a puppy's daily calorie needs decrease as he gets older.*

when the pup is four to five weeks old, and by six to eight weeks he's not nursing any more. Up to the age of four to six months the puppy needs approximately 60 calories a day for every pound of his weight. After six months, there's a fairly rapid decrease in his calorie requirements and by the time he's a year old he will need only about 35 to 40 calories per pound of body weight. Remember, however, that dogs differ in appetite and this is only a guide.

Your eight-week-old puppy must be fed at least three or four times a day. When he starts losing interest in a meal, decrease the number of feedings so that—in the case of most types of dogs—by eight months he's eating once a day. Exceptions to this one-meal-a-day rule are some of the giant breeds, which may require multiple feedings up to and past one year of age. You will be talking to your veterinarian at intervals during this first year, and he will advise on how many feedings your larger dog needs.

When you bring your puppy home, start him on a regular feeding schedule right away; this means feeding at the same times each day. In the first days stay with the type of food the puppy was weaned on—ideally, this should be a good commercial dry puppy food plus additional meat. You can moisten the dry food with water to stimulate the puppy's appetite, but don't make it too soupy. An exception to this may be a very small puppy whose teeth are erupting late and who seems able to handle only moistened food.

The meat you add should account for about 10 percent of the puppy's food intake. You can use a commercial canned meat product for dogs or something as simple as cooked ground beef. As well as this dry food and meat mixture, give the puppy one egg yolk a day—separate the yolk from the white, or use strained egg yolks from the baby food shelf at the grocery store. (You don't give the white of the egg at this stage because it's hard for the puppy to digest.)

When the pup is six months old, replace the daily egg yolk with a whole egg given cooked or raw once a week. Once a day mix some cottage cheese with the dog food—it's a valuable source of protein and minerals. A good vegetable oil added to the food daily is also recommended; it supplies additional fatty acids which help keep the dog's coat healthy.

Don't, however, swamp your new puppy with all these nutrients at once. Start with the dry food and meat mixture and add the supplements one at a time until you're sure the puppy's digestive system can tolerate each one. You can judge this tolerance by keeping an eye on the puppy's stools; as long as they're formed, you're on the right track, but if they loosen and stay loose you should withdraw the offending supplement and try again another time. Remember to keep your dog supplied with fresh water at all times. Don't ever deprive the dog of water as a method of training.

ESTABLISHING GOOD EATING HABITS

The amount you feed will vary from one dog to another. As a rule of thumb, follow the manufacturer's recommendations and leave the food bowl down for no longer than 10 to 15 minutes. When the puppy walks away, assume he's had enough and pick the food up. If he gobbles up the food and looks around for more, give him some more. If the puppy walks away from the bowl without eating, don't assume that he doesn't like the cuisine and offer him something else. Remember that you're the boss and you set the schedule. If he rejects the food when you put it down, remove it until the next meal. Don't give in if he looks hungry ten minutes later, and don't offer him table food—this will just establish life-long bad habits and let him know that he can manipulate you to feed him on demand. Make it clear that if he doesn't eat on schedule, he can go hungry. A healthy puppy will soon learn that he'd better eat when food is offered rather than suffer those hunger pains. You can make it easier on yourself by feeding the puppy at the same time that you eat and not offering him table food.

Should you give your puppy vitamins? As a rule the answer is no. Vitamins are not usually necessary if the puppy is getting a balanced diet. You can, if you wish, give him a veterinary vitamin supplement during the first months when he's growing fast, but if you're feeding him a good quality dog food it should be supplying all the vitamins and minerals he needs.

A word of warning: Despite what you may have heard, rapidly growing large breeds do not need additional calcium and phosphorus provided they are getting a balanced daily diet. Your veterinarian can tell you that a lot of the bone problems seen in veterinary practice are due to over-supplementation of calcium, phosphorus, and vitamin D.

Do remember that for all breeds of dogs the most rapid growth occurs in the first six months, and adequate nutrition during this time is essential to healthy development. Of course, the pup continues to grow after six months, but the rate of growth is slower and his nutritional requirements slow down.

DAILY CALORIE REQUIREMENTS
FOR ADULT DOGS

Weight		Calories Per Day
2.3 kgs	5 lbs	140
4.5	10	280
9.1	20	560
13.6	30	840
18.2	40	1120
22.7	50	1400
27.3	60	1680
31.8	70	1960
36.4	80	1900
40.9	90	2160
45.5	100	2400

□ *These figures are based on the results of scientific studies on dog nutrition and represent the requirements of a medium to large house dog.*

□ *Active or working dogs may require 40 to 50% more calories than this chart depicts. Outside dogs and pregnant or lactating dogs need 30 to 50% more calories.*

□ *The larger the dog, the fewer the daily calories required. For large breeds (breeds weighing more than 70 lbs. adult weight) reduce the above figures by 10%.*

FEEDING THE ADULT DOG

Once your dog is fully grown, he usually does very well on one meal a day unless he belongs to one of the large, deep-chested breeds like the St. Bernard or Great Dane. If they eat too much at one time these dogs can develop bloat—an accumulation of gas in the stomach which puts severe pressure on the internal organs. Bloat is a very serious and frequently fatal condition, and in order to avoid it, susceptible breeds should be fed several small meals a day instead of one large meal.

If you're feeding your dog once a day, the most convenient time is probably in the evening when you have your own dinner—this also discourages table-begging. The time you feed, however depends on your convenience and your personal schedule. Don't ever succumb to that hungry look in your dog's eyes (he's faking) and give table scraps. You can end up with a fat dog or a dog with stomach and intestinal problems.

The quantity you feed a grown dog depends partly on his activity level. A dog that lies around the house most of the day may need up to 30 percent fewer calories than a very active dog.

The diet for the adult dog is very similar to that of the puppy—a good quality dry or semi-moist dog food with additional meat (up to 10 percent of the total) for extra high-quality protein. A sensible general rule is to take the manufacturer's recommended quantity according to the body weight of your dog, then reduce that quantity by about 10 percent. But use your common sense. If your dog is gaining weight, decrease the quantity of food. If he's losing weight, increase it. Remember, however, that a dog that's a bit hungry is healthier than a dog that's so full he can't walk away from the food bowl.

What about supplements to your dog's basic diet? Continue to add a good quality vegetable oil to his food as you did when he was a puppy. This provides fatty acids to the skin and prevents drying of the coat. Add one teaspoonful of oil for each 10 pounds of the dog's weight up to a maximum of two tablespoons. If the oil makes the dog's stool loose, discontinue it and ask your veterinarian for a supplement to give instead.

It's okay to give your dog an occasional treat between meals, but give only dog treats and remember that they have calories. A dog that's getting too many treats in addition to his regular diet will soon put on weight.

Contrary to what you may have been told, dogs don't need bones. Your dog's wild ancestors gnawed on bones because they needed the minerals that bones contain. A well-balanced commercial dog food already contains all the necessary minerals. Feeding bones to your dog is asking for trouble; bones can cause constipation, intestinal obstruction, and broken teeth. It's also a fallacy that chewing on bones is necessary to keep the dog's teeth clean and healthy. If you want to give him something to chew on, choose a hard rubber toy or a rawhide or synthetic bone.

If old habits die so hard that you still want to give the dog a bone, make it a beef marrow or shank bone and don't let the dog break the bone up. Don't ever feed the dog soft bones like chicken or ribs that can catch in the throat and choke the animal.

FEEDING AN AGING DOG

As your dog ages, all his functions slow down. He sleeps more and takes less exercise. His kidneys begin to scar up and become unable to handle excessive protein. At this stage you need to adjust the dog's diet by decreasing the amount of protein but increasing its quality. This can be accomplished by cutting down on dog treats which frequently contain poor quality protein.

If your dog develops heart disease as he gets older, a low-salt diet is indicated. Other disorders such as kidney disease, liver disease, or intestinal and stomach problems all require special dietary adaptations. As a rule, you should have your veterinarian recommend a suitable diet for an aging dog on the basis of the dog's general health.

If your veterinarian recommends a special diet he will probably direct you to one of the commercially prepared foods that can be purchased only through a veterinarian. These are a bit more expensive than regular dog foods because they call for more expensive ingredients. A special diet formulated for dogs with food allergies, for instance, is made up of lamb and rice plus the necessary vitamins and minerals. The lamb adds to the expense, but it's used because very few dogs are allergic to lamb. You can make up a special diet for your dog at home, according to the veterinarian's recommendations, but you'll probably discover that the cost is no less than that of a commercial special food.

When your dog needs special feeding, you'll find it in your favor that you've raised him with good table manners. Dogs that have never become accustomed to commercial dog foods will balk at a commercially prepared special diet—thus requiring the owner to spend a lot of time in the kitchen fixing just what the veterinarian ordered.

Another word of warning: If your dog is on a special diet, don't feed him anything else without the approval of your veterinarian.

THE WELL-BEHAVED DOG

The well-behaved dog needs to learn more than just to be clean in the house. As your companion, your dog will go places and meet people with you and you will expect him to behave in a socially acceptable way on these occasions. Training your dog to be a pleasure to have around can begin, in small but practical ways, as soon as he becomes part of your family. Later, you may decide you want to take him to obedience training classes. If your dog is a puppy, however, obedience classes should wait until he's at least six months old. Although there are some puppy classes available, most will not accept a dog under the age of six months. Like small children, puppies have a short attention span and are too busy playing to be bothered with appropriate behavior.

All the same, you can prepare your puppy for training even when he's small by introducing him to the commands you'll expect him to obey when he's older, and by using a firm voice and consistent behavior to get him accustomed to what you expect from him. For instance, you can call the pup's name and say "come." It's best to do this when you know he wants to come to you anyway, so that you can reinforce his good behavior by praising him. The full message may not get to him right away, but you're laying the groundwork for future obedience training.

OBEDIENCE: MORE THAN CUTE TRICKS

Some dog owners think it's cute to teach their dogs to roll over, sit up and beg, fetch the newspaper, or do other tricks. But that's not what obedience training is about. Obedience training teaches the dog to listen to your command, to obey when the command is given, and then to wait for the next

Training your dog is important for sociability and safety. Basic obedience training teaches him to sit, stay, walk at heel, and come on command.

command. Take an untrained, exuberant dog for a walk and he may try to pull you across a busy road against the lights. But if your dog is properly trained he will obey your order to halt and sit at the curb, and will then cross the street politely at your side when you give the command—a gentle pull at the leash is often enough.

There are many practical advantages of obedience training. A trained dog won't jump all over strangers (you may think it's okay to have him jump up, but not everyone likes dogs); he won't bark unnecessarily and infuriate the neighbors; he won't trample over other people's yards and chase their cats. He may well want to do all those things, but your command will stop him.

And, of course, training your dog is an important safety measure as well as a social one. A dog that's not trained to behave on busy streets is likely to end up the victim of a road accident.

If you have a very receptive dog you may be able to train him quite adequately yourself, perhaps with the help of an instruction manual. Usually, however, you'll get better results from taking the dog to obedience classes. Moreover, you'll enjoy the classes too—they're inexpensive, they're fun, they're rewarding, and you get to see how other people and their dogs get along.

Most beginning obedience classes run for 10 or 12 weeks and require your presence with your dog one night a week. Between classes, you're expected to practice with the dog at home. Your dog should learn to perform basic tasks calmly at the first command—to sit, stay, walk at heel, come on command, and so on. You can ask your veterinarian to recommend a class, or look for advertisements in the local newspaper. Remember, however, that the only right way to train a dog is with firm, consistent, and gentle handling. Harsh punishment is never appropriate, and you should never let your dog be part of any class where you feel that the trainer is mistreating the animals or encouraging training methods other than those based on kindness.

Most dogs thoroughly enjoy obedience work and take to it at once. And, as you and your dog learn together, you may find that you want to continue to more advanced obedience training. If your dog is a purebred, you may even reach the point where he can show off his paces in obedience trials where, unlike regular conformation shows, the criteria for success are based on brains, not beauty.

A word here on formal training, such as that undergone by dogs that work for a living as guard dogs, police dogs, or guide dogs for the blind. Training for all these animals is carried out by professionals, and is a far more lengthy and involved process than that of obedience training a family dog. Police dogs and guide dogs are generally trained by, or in close cooperation with, the person who will handle them after training. Guard dogs are usually left at a facility for training, then the owner is in turn trained how to handle the dog. Although your dog may do a good job of protecting your property by barking at intruders or intimidating them by his presence, it is not usually wise to expect a professionally trained guard dog to double as a family pet.

THE WELL-TRAVELED DOG

A dog that has been obedience trained probably makes a better traveling companion than an untrained dog, and most owners travel with their dogs at some time or another—even if it's only to the veterinarian's office or to the grooming establishment for trimming or bathing. In fact, both of these trips are surefire anxiety producers for the dog and, if he doesn't particularly care for the car anyway, you're in for a miserable trip. Dogs that are inexperienced travelers frequently suffer from motion sickness which makes them drool or vomit; this is more often true of younger animals but it does occur in adult dogs too. You can, however, take practical steps while the dog is still young or a newcomer in your home to forestall motion sickness. Here's a simple program for getting your dog used to the car:

- Sit in your parked car with your dog for a few minutes

each day. Talk to your dog to make him feel comfortable, but don't start the car.

• After a couple of days, repeat the procedure but start up the car. Don't drive anywhere; just praise the dog.

• After a few more days, put the dog where you want him to sit while traveling (in the back seat, for instance), start up the car, and drive around the block. If possible, go to a park or some other setting that will help the dog associate car travel with a pleasant outcome.

• Repeat this drill daily, increasing the distance you drive each day. With any luck at all, your dog will soon be acting like a seasoned traveler.

If these tactics don't work and your dog is consistently car sick, ask the veterinarian to prescribe medication for the dog before you take a trip.

There are several other important considerations to keep in mind when you take your dog in the car:

• Never let your dog sit on your lap while you're driving, and make sure large dogs stay in the back seat.

• Never let your dog hang his head out of the car window while the car's moving; the air blowing against his eyes can cause conjunctivitis (severe irritation of the tissue around the eyes).

• Never leave a dog unattended in a closed car on a hot day. The most common cause of heat prostration (often fatal) in dogs is overheating in an automobile. If you must leave the dog in the car, park the car in the shade and leave the windows partially open. However, don't leave the dog unless it's absolutely necessary; an excited dog in a closed hot car can overheat in just a few minutes and brain damage follows very quickly.

AIR TRAVEL: CHECKING REGULATIONS

Specific regulations apply to dogs traveling by air or on other forms of public transportation, and you should always check these out before a trip. Airlines require that the dog be enclosed in a travel kennel or crate. If the crate is small enough to go under your seat in the aircraft, the dog can travel with you; otherwise, the animal must travel in the baggage compartment. The baggage compartment is pressurized and the temperature controlled, so your dog will come to no harm (beyond, probably, being lonely and somewhat apprehensive).

Most airlines sell dog crates, and all you need to do is make sure that the crate is large enough for your dog to stand, turn, and lie down comfortably. Attach identification both to the crate and to the dog's collar, and attach to the crate copies of any health certification required by the state or foreign country to which the dog is traveling.

Your veterinarian can tell you what certification you need if you're taking your dog out of state, and be sure to get this information well ahead of time especially if you're traveling to a foreign country. In this case, contact the consulate for that country and have then send you the appropriate forms. Frequently your state Department of Agriculture will have to approve the documents—another good reason for not leaving it until the last minute.

Wherever you're traveling, take your dog to the veterinarian at least two weeks before your departure date. The veterinarian will make sure all the dog's vaccinations are up to date, review the dog's medical condition, and, in some cases, prescribe a tranquilizer to calm the dog and counteract motion sickness.

VACATIONING WITH YOUR DOG

It's quite possible to take your dog on vacation with you, but it requires both common sense and advance planning. First of all, be sure that the place you plan to stay at won't turn you away when you arrive with a dog in tow. Some hotel or motel chains publish directories listing which of their facilities allow dogs. Call the facility nearest to your home for information. Your local library is also a useful source of information. If you plan to camp, check on the regulations that apply at the campgrounds you wish to stay at. Again, you can get this information from directories available in most public libraries, or direct from the campgrounds.

Remember that the change of environment and general excitement of vacation time may affect a dog in unexpected ways. Your normally well-behaved dog may become a noisy, nervous problem and this will not only wreck your vacation but make you unpopular with others at your motel or campground. You can minimize these adjustment problems by taking along familiar objects like the dog's food dish, bedding, or toys; giving him lots of reassurance; and discouraging strangers who are over-eager to pet him. If you are not confident that your dog can handle a vacation away from home, it's best to make arrangements for his care and leave him behind.

THE STAY-AT-HOME DOG

If, for one reason or another it's not possible to take your dog with you on a trip, you have the options of either having the dog cared for in your own home, sending him to a boarding kennel, or (if the dog is adaptable) having him stay with a friend or neighbor he knows well.

In many urban areas it's possible to find "dog sitters" who will care for the dog in your home. Your veterinarian may be able to recommend someone, or sitters may advertise in the local press. If the sitter is someone you don't know, be sure to check references.

If you decide to board your dog in a kennel, get recommendations from your friends or the veterinarian and, if possible, visit several kennels before you make your choice. Look for cleanliness and a caring staff, and don't patronize any kennel that seems reluctant to have you tour the facility—reputable establishments are always happy to show you around. The American Boarding Kennels Association (ABKA) makes available a list of member establishments along with advice on how to select a boarding kennel. You can write to the ABKA at 311 N. Union, Colorado Springs, CO 80909. Once you've decided on a boarding kennel, make the reservation as early as possible—good kennels fill up fast especially at vacation time.

Before you leave your pet in the care of anyone—friend or professional—make sure the person is fully aware of the animal's feeding schedule, habits, fears and idiosyncrasies, and so on. Make sure the dog's vaccinations are current, and leave the phone numbers of your veterinarian and emergency service. Then you can enjoy your trip in the confidence that your dog will be well cared for in your absence.

GROOMING: THE GOOD-LOOKING DOG

Good grooming is as important to your dog as it is to you. A well-groomed dog looks good and feels good, and grooming sessions serve two useful purposes beyond the obvious goal of cleanliness: they are (or should be) fun for you both, and they give you a chance to do a quick check on your dog's general health.

Grooming involves caring not only for the dog's coat, but also for the eyes, ears, nails, and anal sacs. The amount of grooming your dog needs depends a lot on the breed—and you'll have taken this into account before you took the dog into your home.

Combing and brushing are the first steps to keeping your dog well-groomed. Combing separates the tangled hair at skin level; brushing removes dead hair and gives luster to the coat. Long-haired dogs like poodles, Yorkshire terriers, Maltese terriers, Lhasa apsos, Old English sheepdogs, and so on, need to be combed and brushed frequently, sometimes every day, to prevent the hair from becoming matted. And the longer the hair, the more work it is for you. A short-haired dog usually won't need combing at all because the hair doesn't often tangle or mat. For these dogs, a good brushing is adequate.

Not all dogs take kindly to the grooming process, but most of them love the attention and the good feeling that they get from being groomed—just as you feel good after a shower or a visit to the beauty shop. And the best way to insure that grooming is fun for you both is to start with short, daily sessions when the dog is a puppy. The easiest way to groom a puppy or a small dog is on a table, so that you won't have to stoop. Just being on a raised surface will probably make the dog a bit nervous so he'll stay still instead of bouncing around and complicating things. A slippery surface, though, may upset him thoroughly and is dangerous because the dog may skid and fall. Put a rubber mat on the table to give him a good footing and help him feel secure.

Make the first grooming sessions short—just a few minutes a day—and heap your dog with praise at the end of each successful session. Tell him how proud you are of him and how beautiful he looks. Pretty soon he'll be looking forward to grooming sessions and the approval that accompanies them. Don't give up if your early attempts to groom your puppy are frustrating. Stick with it, take it slowly, and don't lose your temper.

As your dog gets used to being groomed, make sure that you handle all parts of his body during the process. Look at his eyes and ears; open his mouth and run your fingers along his gums. This way the dog will get used to your touch and you'll have a much easier job when the time comes to give him medication or inspect or clean his teeth.

If you happen to have a dog that—despite all your care and approval—hates to be touched, you'll have to use different tactics. You may need to recruit another family member to hold the dog while you groom him. You may even have to restrain the dog with a muzzle. Don't let up on the praise, though, when he does behave. You don't often come across a dog that can't be persuaded to at least tolerate being groomed.

If, however, you do find that you've become the owner of a dog that won't let you groom him adequately— perhaps you've adopted an older dog that never had a chance to get used to this socializing activity, or a dog that has been abused and is consequently hand shy—you'll need to rely on professional care. Ask your veterinarian to recommend a grooming establishment.

GROOMING EQUIPMENT

The following equipment should be all you need to keep your dog looking good.

Brush and comb. If you've got a short-haired dog, use a medium soft brush to keep his coat in shape. He'll find it very comforting, too, provided you remember always to brush in the direction of growth. With a long-haired dog you'll need first to use a comb to separate the tangled hair, then a firm bristle brush.

It's important to choose the right brush, and the best kind for all-round use is a soft wire slicker brush which is between the very soft brushes used on show dogs and the harsh slicker brushes sold in many pet stores. Natural bristle brushes are good, but they don't remove the dead hair nearly as effectively as the slicker brush. If the dog's coat is badly matted, a Universal brush (like a slicker brush but convex in shape) removes the mats much better than a slicker brush. When you're buying a comb for your dog, choose one that has half fine and half coarse teeth. The illustration on page 63 shows some of the grooming aids available in pet stores.

Scissors. With some breeds, such as poodles and Lhasa apsos, you'll need scissors to trim away hair around the eyes so that it won't get in the eyes and cause irritation or trap debris that could lead to an infection. You'll also use the scissors to cut away any hair that becomes matted around the rectum. Here, too, matted hair can collect debris and cause irritation or infection.

Nail clippers. It's very important to trim the nails of any dog that doesn't get enough exercise to keep the nails worn down naturally. Don't ever use human nail clippers

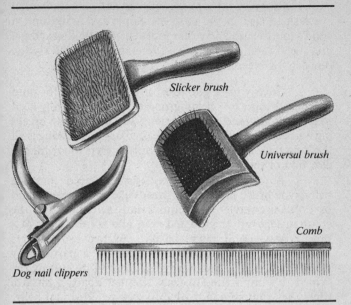

Slicker brush

Universal brush

Comb

Dog nail clippers

on your dog. You can get special dog nail clippers from any pet supplier. If you don't know what to get, ask your veterinarian to recommend a brand.

Shampoo. Your grooming supplies should include either a special dog shampoo or a very mild human product like a "tear-free" baby shampoo. Most human shampoos, however, are much too harsh for a dog's skin. Don't think you're doing your dog a favor, either, by randomly using a product that also kills fleas. Again, these products are very drying and should be used only for the stated purpose—on a dog that has fleas—and on the advice of your veterinarian.

Miscellaneous supplies. Your grooming kit can usefully include a number of other items, many of which you probably already have in your home: Mineral oil, (a drop in each eye before bathing prevents eye irritation); cotton swabs with baby oil for cleaning the ears; a commercial eyewash to use in the case of simple eye irritations; a child's toothbrush and either toothpaste or baking soda—dogs need their teeth cleaned sometimes, too; and styptic powder for bleeding nails.

Once you've got your dog accustomed to—and looking forward to—being groomed, you'll probably need to groom him three or four times a week. Start with brushing and combing. With a short-haired dog, a brushing is all that's needed. Brush firmly but gently, always following the direction of the hair growth.

A long-haired dog will usually need combing before you brush him—some breeds like the Afghan hound or Yorkshire terrier will require daily attention. Use the comb to separate the tangled hair, and comb a little at a time. Always comb from the skin out, because the mats form at skin level. Don't try to cut off a particularly stubborn mat; you'll almost certainly end up cutting the skin. If it's impossible to tease the mat apart, a bit at a time, then you should probably seek professional help.

One advantage of regular grooming is that it cuts down the amount of loose hair you'll have to vacuum off the rug or the sofa. Certain breeds, like German shepherds, Norwegian elkhounds, collies, and Pomeranians have a double coat. The undercoat is very soft and tends to trap loose hair, so regular (preferably daily) brushing with a stiff brush will remove this loose hair and keep it off your clothes and furniture.

Some breeds need professional grooming on a regular basis, especially if the animal is a show dog. Certain breeds such as schnauzers, Kerry blue terriers, and Scottish terriers, have to be trimmed to American Kennel Club breed standards before they can be exhibited, and unless you are experienced at this, it's best to leave the job to a professional. This need for professional beauty treatments should be something you took into consideration before you bought the dog. Ask you veterinarian to recommend a good professional grooming establishment.

BATHING: WHEN AND WHEN NOT TO BATHE A DOG

It should not be necessary to bathe your dog more than once a month—a short-haired dog that leads a conservative indoor life won't need bathing even that often. Too frequent bathing is not only unnecessary but inadvisable—it robs the skin of its natural protective oils and causes it to become dry and scaly.

Don't make the mistake of bathing your dog just because "he smells." Dogs are supposed to have an odor—though not an offensive one—and any unusually noticeable odor may mean something quite different from straightforward grubbiness. If there's a strong odor coming from your dog, check the mouth, ears, and anal sacs. Dental problems can cause a strong odor which may seem to you to be coming from the whole dog, not just the mouth. Ear infections give off a musty smell which is immediately recognizable once you know what you're looking for. A strong, persistent odor coming from the anal sacs can indicate an infection. Don't bathe your dog to cover up any of these odors; they all require specialized treatment or veterinary attention.

If you've decided that your dog does need a bath, make sure you've got room to do the job. The bathtub is fine for most smaller dogs. As with regular grooming on the table top, a rubber mat in the tub will stop the animal from slipping around and getting panicky. If you've got a very large dog, your best bet may be to bathe him in the backyard and get the shampoo off with the garden hose. In this case, choose a warm, sunny day so that the dog will not get chilled by the cold water from the hose and will dry off quickly in the sun. If you're bathing the dog indoors, use lukewarm water—never too hot or too cold—and fill the bathtub or other container to the level of the dog's elbows. An alternative method is to use a shower hose attached to the faucet.

Before putting the dog into the water, make sure all the knots and tangles are combed out of his coat. Place a

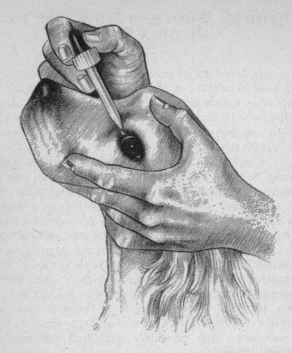

A drop of mineral oil in the corner of each eye prevents irritation from soap at bath time.

drop of mineral oil in the inner corner of each eye (use a dropper) to protect against irritation from the soap, and a wad of cotton in each ear to stop water getting in the ears. Wet the dog thoroughly and pour a small amount of the dog or baby shampoo you're using down his back. Vigorously massage the shampoo down to the skin, taking care to wash under the tail, the legs, and the abdomen. Rinse the shampoo off thoroughly so that there's no soap residue to cause irritation later. Let the dog shake to get the excess water out of his coat (this is where it's a real advantage to do the whole thing outdoors), then towel him dry.

If the dog is small enough and can tolerate the noise, you can finish drying him with your hair dryer—the blow kind. This may, however, drive him crazy. If he will let you use a blow dryer, use the *warm* setting only. All the time you're drying the dog, talk to him soothingly and praise him lavishly so that the bath he regards as a big pain seems a bit more pleasurable.

If you can't, for some reason, wet bathe your dog, you can try one of the commercial dry dog shampoos that are on the market. Massage the shampoo into the coat according to the directions, then brush it out. A dry shampoo can do a reasonably good job, but it's no substitute for a real wet bath.

When you're bathing your dog you have the ideal opportunity for checking out the skin all over the body for any irritations or lesions that may need attention. At this time check also for ticks and fleas. If you find them, deal with them as discussed in the section on parasites.

GENERAL HEALTH CARE AT GROOMING TIME

Whether you're bathing your dog or just brushing and combing him, part of the grooming session should include attention to the eyes, ears, nails, teeth, and anal sacs.

A healthy dog's eyes should always be bright and shining, with wide open lids. Occasionally the eyes may seem mildly irritated, in which case you can apply a commercial, nonmedicated eyewash. When you're grooming the dog, gently wipe away any discharge that has accumulated in the corners of the eyes. If there's a green or yellow discharge, call your veterinarian. This is particularly important if the discharge is accompanied by redness of the eyes. Another cause for veterinary attention is excessive tearing; the veterinarian will check that the tear ducts are functioning properly. White-haired dogs that tear a lot develop brown stains on the fur between the corners of the eyes and the mouth. Provided that the veterinarian has determined that the tearing is normal, there's nothing you can do about the discoloration. It's unsightly, but you have to put up with it.

Clean your dog's ears routinely, once a week. Cleaning is particularly important if the dog has floppy ears which keep the ear canal moist and prevent air circulation. This type of ear fosters the growth of bacteria and yeast, which are major causes of canine ear infections.

Clean the ears with a cotton swab dipped in baby oil. The long ear canal is L-shaped, going straight down and then turning in toward the head. At the end of the L is the eardrum. To clean the ear, hold the ear flap (or pinna) straight up above the head and gently place the swab into the canal in a vertical position; that is, facing down toward the floor. This way the swab can't enter far enough into the canal to harm the eardrum.

Some dogs, like poodles, grow hair in their ears, and if this hair is not removed it can cause infection. Superficial hair can be removed easily: grasp it with your fingers and pluck it out. Deeper hair must be removed by a veterinarian, and so must any hair on an area of the ear which appears to be red or irritated. If there's an unpleasant odor from the dog's ears, or if he scratches at the ear or tilts his head persistently to one side, call the veterinarian.

Wild canines get enough exercise on hard ground to keep their nails worn down to the right length—just touching the ground but no longer. Large domestic dogs that get plenty of energetic outdoor exercise usually wear down their nails naturally. Small dogs that spend most of their time indoors, however, need their nails cut. And shaggy dogs with long hair on their feet (like cocker spaniels, Shih Tzus, and pulis) may deceive you into thinking their nails are not too long; look again.

Trimming a dog's nails is not as easy as it sounds. The process is simple, but the dog's reaction often turns it into a major production—he puts up a big fuss, and fidgets and complains so that it's hard for you to get to grips with the job.

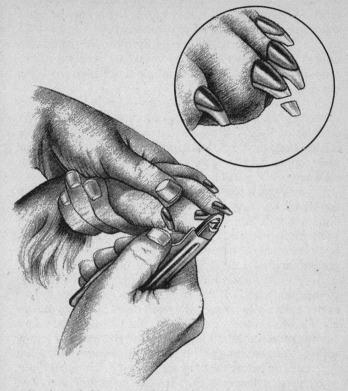

Use dog nail clippers–never human clippers–and cut the dog's nails above the point where the nail starts to curve downward.

Before cutting the nails, look carefully to make sure you know what you're doing. Each nail has a blood vessel and a nerve—the quick. If you cut into the quick, you'll hurt the dog and cause bleeding. If the dog has white or pale nails, you can see the quick as the pink line running in the nail. Using the special dog nail clippers described earlier, cut the nail a little above the quick as shown in the accompanying illustration. If the dog's nails are black, your task is more difficult; clip a little at a time to be sure you don't cut into the quick. A generally safe rule is to cut just below the point where the nail starts to curve downwards.

If you accidently cut the quick, don't panic—although your dog will certainly complain. Apply a styptic powder or pencil to the cut, or apply direct pressure to the bleeding nail for five minutes.

How short should you clip the nails? As short as you safely can without drawing blood. And how often? As often as necessary. The more often you clip the nails, the further back the quick will grow. Eventually you'll get the nails clipped back to where they don't touch the ground at all when the dog is standing straight.

When you're trimming the nails, don't forget to clip the dewclaws, which are equivalent to the nails on the human thumb. Some dogs have dewclaws on both front and back feet; some don't have any at all because they were removed when the dog was a puppy. These never touch the ground, and have no chance to wear down.

Even conscientious owners often overlook the care of their dog's teeth. If you have a puppy, watch for him to begin replacing his front baby teeth when he's three or four months old. At this time, you may see blood on the gums, empty spaces, or double teeth. It's unlikely that your puppy will have any teething problems, but occasionally the adult teeth come in before the baby teeth fall out. In this case your veterinarian will correct the situation before the dog's bite (the way the top and bottom teeth close together) is affected.

The teeth of adult dogs often develop stains and dental calculus, commonly called tartar—the deposits located on the teeth at the gumline. If tartar is allowed to accumulate it will cause bacteria to form under the gum, and this will lead to pyorrhea (which is the accumulation of pus along the root of the tooth) and eventual tooth loss. Mouth odor is a sure sign of decay, infection, or a dietary problem, so any time your dog has "bad breath," have your veterinarian check it out.

If you have children, you probably figure you have enough trouble getting the kids to brush their teeth without having to worry about the dog, too. Regular toothbrushing, however, will do wonders to help keep your dog's mouth healthy. Use a child's toothbrush dipped in baking soda (or regular toothpaste) and rub the teeth and gums vigorously. Remember that a hard food diet and suitable toys to chew on—hard rubber or rawhide playthings, for instance—help somewhat to keep your dog's teeth in good shape. Do not, however, give a dog meat bones; they can splinter and injure the dog.

Care of the anal sacs should be part of every grooming. These sacs are located immediately under the

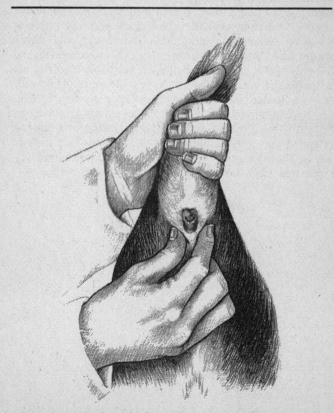

Blocked anal glands can lead to problems like infection and irritation.
Make sure the glands are emptied regularly.

rectum at the five o'clock and seven o'clock positions, and were originally used for marking out the dog's territory in the wild state. The odor of the material emitted from the anal sacs is very unpleasant. Normally, the sacs empty automatically each time the dog has a bowel movement, but variations in the diet and consequently in the consistency of the stool can impede this natural regulation.

By making sure the sacs are emptied regularly you can avoid impaction, infection, and rectal irritation in the dog. To relieve blocked anal glands, take the dog's tail in one hand and raise it as shown in the illustration on the previous page. Using a paper towel, place the index finger and thumb of your free hand over the five o'clock and seven o'clock positions respectively, and press the thumb and finger inward and then toward each other. This squeezes out the contents of the glands. Your dog will probably object to this procedure, so you may want to have someone hold his head.

Sometimes home treatment may not be effective, and a veterinarian has to squeeze the glands internally to empty them. If your dog is scooting (sitting with his tail extended and moving along the floor on his rear end) or showing other signs of discomfort that are not relieved by home treatment, take him to the veterinarian's office.

VACCINATION: A KEY TO GOOD HEALTH

Just as vaccinations now protect children from conditions that used to be killers, scientists have discovered ways to vaccinate dogs against a number of once fatal diseases. Vaccinations are a routine part of your preventative medicine schedule for your dog, and the first time you meet your veterinarian on a professional basis will probably be when you take your puppy for these shots.

In both humans and animals, the body is protected against disease by substances called antibodies that are carried in the white blood cells. These antibodies form in response to the presence of a specific disease-causing microorganism in the body, and are able to fight and kill the invader.

One way to develop immunity is to contract a disease and recover from it. Since this is neither practical or desirable, vaccination is used to protect against some diseases.

Vaccination involves injecting into the body a vaccine—a preparation containing the microorganism that caues the disease against which protection is required. The

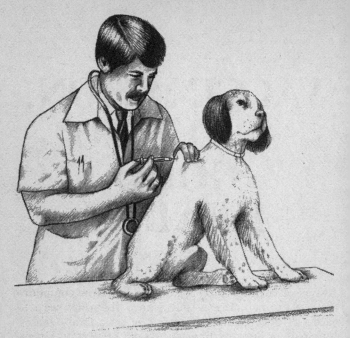

*Vaccination is now available to protect dogs against a number
of diseases that used to be killers. The veterinarian begins
the vaccination schedule when the dog is a puppy; regular booster
shots maintain the protection for life.*

microorganism in the vaccine, however, has been biologi-
cally altered so that it cannot actually cause disease. The
body responds to the vaccine as if the disease were present,
and forms protective antibodies to fight it. This protection,
in some cases, can last a lifetime. In other cases, the vaccination must be repeated at intervals (usually annually) to
maintain its effect.

Don't assume that because you plan for your dog to
lead a sheltered life, he doesn't need to be vaccinated. Veterinarians hear this all too often, and point out that a bigger
myth couldn't exist. The best analogy is that of a bed-ridden

person who lives alone and who never leaves the house, yet still gets sick. The viruses and bacteria that cause illness in both people and in dogs are easily spread either in the air or on shoes and clothing, and no dog is safe from diseases like canine distemper unless he has received the appropriate vaccination.

All puppies receive a certain amount of natural immunity to disease from their mother. The protective antibodies are passed to the puppies in the first milk—or colostrum—in the first 24 hours of life. This protection, however, is short-lived, depending in part on how well-protected the mother was before the birth of the litter. Some puppies receive very little protection and are susceptible to disease as early as six to eight weeks after birth; most puppies lose all this acquired immunity by the time they are 14 to 16 weeks old. The veterinarian, therefore, starts vaccinating puppies when they're between six and eight weeks old. Your veterinarian will work out a suitable schedule for your particular dog, and the complete program will cover the following infectious diseases:

> *Distemper*
> *Hepatitis* (adenovirus type 1 or type 2)
> *Leptospirosis*
> *Parvovirus*
> *Rabies*
> *Canine respiratory disease* (kennel cough)

Note that vaccination is effective against only three of the many possible causes of kennel cough, so the dog receives only partial protection.

These diseases are explained below.

DISTEMPER

Distemper is a highly contagious viral disease of dogs. Contrary to popular opinion, it has nothing to do with the dog's temperament or personality. It's caused by a virus, related to the human measles virus, that the dog contracts either by inhaling it from the air or by direct contact with an infected dog. The virus incubates in the dog for seven to nine days before any signs appear.

Signs and diagnosis. The first signs of distemper are commonly lethargy and an unusually high temperature—103° to 105°F. If the dog has no immunity to the disease, the virus infects the whole body causing a second rise in temperature along with signs of severe physical weakness, lack of appetite, discharge from the eyes and nose, cough, pneumonia, and—in many cases—diarrhea. Because these symptoms may also be indicative of other conditions, careful diagnosis is required. The veterinarian may take blood samples in order to make the diagnosis. The distemper virus also attacks the brain and can lead to convulsions and death.

Unfortunately, it sometimes happens that none of the early signs of distemper are recognized by the owner, and no action is taken until the dog shows signs of neurological damage—convulsions, jerking movements of the head and jaws, and inability to stand. If these occur, it may be necessary to euthanize the dog. If the dog survives, he may be left with permanent but acceptable neurological disturbances, like jerking movements of the head or legs. The dog, however, functions normally in every other way.

Treatment. Because distemper is caused by a virus, treatment is seldom effective. Occasionally supportive therapy—good nursing care and careful feeding—and antibiotics for secondary infection will enable the dog to survive this very dangerous disease. Among other medications the veterinarian may prescribe are antidiarrheals, cough medicines, anti-convulsants, and intravenous fluids.

Prevention. If the female dog is properly vaccinated before she is bred, she will impart good temporary immunity to the puppies. The puppies must then be vaccinated at six to eight weeks, and twice more up to 16 weeks of age. Puppies must be kept away from older, unvaccinated dogs until the vaccination program is complete. Older dogs must receive booster shots each year in order to be fully protected. And remember that distemper is not just a "puppy disease"—it can affect dogs of all ages.

HEPATITIS (ADENOVIRUS TYPE 1)

Infectious hepatitis is usually caused by canine adenovirus type 1. The virus primarily affects the liver, and all members of the canine family are susceptible. It can affect dogs of any age but is most serious in the young. The virus is transmitted in the urine, stool, or saliva of an infected dog, and the incubation period before symptoms of the disease appear is six to nine days.

Signs and diagnosis.   This disease can appear in many forms, but the most common signs are a rise in temperature ($103°$F/$39°$C to $105°$F/$40.5°$C) lethargy, loss of appetite, tonsillitis, and possibly discharge from the eyes or nose similar to that seen with distemper. Very often the owner does not even realize the dog is sick until he or she notices a cloudiness in the cornea of one or both eyes; this condition is known as "blue eye," and is a sign that the dog is recovering from the virus. However, "blue eye"—edema or swelling of the cornea—can be a dangerous condition in its own right because it can cause blindness, and it requires immediate veterinary attention.

Treatment.   Because hepatitis is caused by a virus, no specific treatment is effective but, as with distemper, antibiotics for secondary infection and good nursing care will usually help the dog to full recovery. The veterinarian may prescribe extra vitamins, a special diet with lots of fluids, even blood transfusions. It's important to note that even when the dog is fully recovered, the hepatitis virus will be present in the urine for several months and may thus be transferred to healthy dogs.

Prevention.   Temporary hepatitis immunity is transferred to the puppies from the mother, but only if she has been adequately vaccinated before the birth of the litter. Hepatitis vaccine is usually combined with the distemper vaccine and given at the same time—when the puppies are six to eight weeks old, and twice more until 16 weeks. Thereafter the dog must get a booster shot every year.

It's appropriate here to talk about adenovirus type 2, and its use in protection against hepatitis. As mentined earlier, infectious hepatitis is usually caused by adenovirus type 1. The type 2 virus, a very close relative of type 1, protects against type 1 infections (hepatitis itself) and against the common upper respiratory infection commonly caused by the type 2 virus. The real advantage of the type 2 vaccination is that it doesn't cause the eye problems that can result from the type 1 vaccine, and it's possible that in the future all infectious hepatitis vaccines will be type 2.

LEPTOSPIROSIS

This is a serious bacterial disease that affects dogs, rats, cattle, and human beings. Because of the possibility of human infection, leptospirosis is regarded as a public health hazard. Two strains of leptospira bacteria can cause the disease in dogs. The bacteria primarily attack the kidneys. The disease is transmitted by direct contact with the urine of an infected animal.

Signs and diagnosis.   A number of warning signs can indicate that the dog has leptospirosis. The most frequent signs are weakness, lack of appetite, high fever, vomiting, and diarrhea. The dog's urine may be a deep yellow color, and he may have mouth ulcers—red patches on the tongue and the edges of the gums. Accurate diagnosis is essential to successful treatment. In addition to noting the signs listed above, the veterinarian may run blood tests to help confirm the diagnosis.

Treatment.   Once the diagnosis is made, leptospirosis can be treated with antibiotics such as penicillin and streptomycin. The dog will need careful nursing, and if he has become dehydrated, it may be necessary to rehydrate him with fluids administered intravenously. Vitamins are usually prescribed to help recovery.

Prevention.   A puppy should be vaccinated against leptospirosis first at nine weeks old and again at 14 to 16 weeks. Thereafter, annual booster shots are necessary. If the dog is exposed to leptospirosis the veterinarian may recommend a booster before the year is up. If there's an outbreak of leptospirosis in a kennel, all dogs must be boostered regardless of when they were last vaccinated. Another important preventive measure is rat control—rats carry the bacteria in their urine and the dog can easily be infected by contact with the rat urine.

PARVOVIRUS

The virus group that parvovirus belongs to is not new to scientists, but until recently they didn't know it could affect dogs. So when the virus appeared in the U.S. in 1978, it caught both the scientists and public off guard. Nobody really knows where the canine parvovirus came from, though there is some indication that a mutation of the cat distemper virus (feline parvovirus) produced a new strain that affects dogs. The virus is spread in the stool, and it's been estimated that a single infected stool can carry over a billion particles of the virus. The disease is now found world-wide.

Signs and diagnosis.   Dogs with parvovirus will usually vomit and have diarrhea; the diarrhea frequently is bloody and has an unpleasant odor. Most dogs develop a fever and have a low white blood cell count. The severity of the disease depends on the age of the dog. Puppies are the most susceptible and may become dehydrated and die in a very short time. Parvovirus can also cause heart muscle disease in very young puppies—two to four weeks old. The veterinarian diagnoses parvovirus by running laboratory tests to detect the presence of antibodies in the blood; this is important because diarrhea and vomiting can also be signs of many other conditions. Although parvovirus is particularly dangerous to puppies, it's not unusual for older dogs to develop a mild infection that clears up with very little treatment.

Treatment.   Unfortunately parvovirus, like most viral conditions, does not respond to any specific treatment. Early diagnosis and intensive care are essential if a severely infected dog—especially a puppy—is to survive. Careful nursing is called for, and the dog will certainly need intravenous fluid therapy to counteract dehydration caused by the diarrhea. The infected premises must be cleaned with one part household bleach to 30 parts of water; this will kill the virus.

Prevention.   Although this is a new disease, it can be successfully prevented by vaccination. As with distemper and hepatitis, an adequately vaccinated female dog will provide temporary immunity to the pups; she should be vaccinated before she is bred. The puppies get a series of shots between the ages of nine weeks and 14 to 16 weeks, and annual or semi-annual boosters are necessary for complete protection.

CANINE RESPIRATORY DISEASE COMPLEX

This disease is commonly known as "kennel cough" because of its primary symptom—a dry, deep cough—and its common occurence in kennels or veterinary hospitals where a number of dogs are housed together. The disease can recur year after year, and although it's not usually serious it causes a lot of grief to dog owners, kennel operators, and veterinarians.

It wasn't until fairly recently that scientists learned that kennel cough can be caused by a number of organisms—not just one. Among the viruses and bacteria that have been isolated as causes are adenovirus type 2, parainfluenza virus, canine herpes virus, and the *Bordetella bronchiseptica* bacterium. Because it usually affects the trachea—the windpipe—and the bronchial tubes, kennel cough is often referred to as "tracheobronchitis."

Signs and diagnosis. In its mild form, kennel cough causes a dry, deep cough. Slight pressure on the windpipe can set the dog coughing spasmodically. A more severe form of the disease causes a deep, productive cough often accompanied by nasal and eye discharges. Pneumonia is a possible complication, and if the disease is not diagnosed and treated promptly it can cause death in young dogs. Diagnosis is usually made on the basis of the clinical signs above, because isolating the exact causative organism is expensive and time-consuming.

Treatment. If bacteria are causing the condition, the dog can be successfully treated with antibiotics. If a virus is the culprit, no specific medications are effective. The veterinarian can, however, prescribe cough suppressants to quiet the dog and relieve his discomfort—owners appreciate this, too, because most infected dogs seem to cough more at night.

Prevention. At the moment, veterinarians can vaccinate against three of the many causes of kennel cough. A very effective parainfluenza virus vaccine is commonly given along with the combined shot for distemper, hepatitis, and leptospirosis. The adenovirus type 2 vaccine used to protect against hepatitis also protects against the respiratory disease caused by the type 2 virus. A vaccine is also available against *Bordetella bronchiseptica* bacteria. This can be given once or twice a year, depending on your veterinarian's assessment of need.

These three protective measures can do a lot to cut down on the incidence of kennel cough, and in a kennel additional protection can be provided by proper ventilation and the use of disinfectants that are effective in destroying viruses and bacteria. The veterinarian can recommend products for kennel use. If your dog is going to be in a high exposure situation—around a lot of other dogs at a show or in a boarding kennel—ask your veterinarian's advice on a booster shot to give him extra protection against possible infection.

RABIES

Rabies is the canine disease everyone knows about. It's caused by a virus that affects the brain and while all warm-blooded animals are susceptible, the animals most commonly affected in North America are dogs, cats, bats, foxes, and skunks. The disease is transmitted by direct contact with the saliva of an infected animal. Because humans can be infected by contact with a rabid animal, and because there is no treatment for rabies, domestic animals must by law be vaccinated against the disease. Rabies laws are strictly enforced throughout the United States.

Signs and diagnosis.   In dogs, rabies usually follows a two-stage pattern. The first stage is demonstrated by a change in behavior. For example, a very gentle dog may become noticeably more aggressive. This is followed by either paralysis or viciousness. In the paralytic form, the dog becomes unable to swallow and the lower jaw often drops open. In the vicious or "furious" form the dog will attack anything in its way. Usually a rabid dog is dead within ten days of the appearance of the first symptoms. If a dog is suspected of having rabies, he must be destroyed and his brain checked for presence of the virus; this is the only way of confirming the diagnosis.

Treatment.   If examination of the dog's brain reveals that the animal did have rabies, any person who had been bitten by the dog or exposed to his saliva must undergo rabies shots. The new human diploid rabies vaccine now used in people who have been exposed to a rabid animal replaces the painful series of shots that used to be given. Early intervention is important. If the diploid vaccine is given before signs of rabies appear, the success rate is high. It's possible, but rare, for the vaccine, correctly used, to save the person once signs of the disease are present.

Prevention.   By law, dogs must be vaccinated against rabies first at the age of four months and then either every year or every three years after that. The precise requirements depend on the law in your area, and your veterinarian will tell you what is required. *Note:* If you ever suspect that your dog or any other animal has rabies, try to confine the animal without touching it—*never* touch an animal that may be rabid with your bare hands—and call the proper authorities. Usually it is only necessary to call the law enforcement agency for your district.

UNDERSTANDING YOUR DOG'S VACCINATION RECORD

When you get your puppy's papers from the breeder, or check out the health record your veterinarian gives you when you take a dog for vaccinations, you'll see a whole bunch of abbreviations. What do they mean?

DM   These initials indicate a distemper-measles vaccine given to a very young puppy to impart immediate protection against distemper.

DMP   This is the distemper-measles vaccine plus parainfluenza, which is part of the canine respiratory disease complex commonly known as kennel cough.

DHL   This stands for distemper, hepatitis, and leptospirosis. It's also known as the "3 in 1" shot.

DA_2L This is the same as the DHL except that the A_2 indicates that the vaccine used was the adenovirus type 2 which, as explained in the discussion of hepatitis, protects against both hepatitis and respiratory disease caused by the type 2 virus.

DA_2LP-P This is a frequently used combination and is essentially a "5 in 1" shot. The initials stand for distemper, adenovirus type 2 (against hepatitis), leptospirosis, parainfluenza, and—the final P—parvovirus.

As it becomes possible to vaccinate against more diseases, the abbreviations will certainly become longer and the "3 in 1"—which is already a "5 in 1"—may well become a "9 in 1".

PARASITES THAT BUG YOUR DOG

Parasites are a problem that most dog owners have to deal with at one time or another. Parasites are, by definition, organisms that survive by feeding off another creature, and the two types that may select your dog as their host are external parasites that live in or on the skin or in the ear canals, and internal parasites that inhabit the internal organs—usually the intestines.

External parasites all resemble insects, and some are so small that they cannot be seen with the naked eye and must be put under a microscope for identification. The external parasites most commonly found on dogs are fleas, ticks, lice, mange mites, and ear mites. Most of them are highly contagious and if one dog in a household is infected, other dogs in the same household are likely to be infected too. These parasites cause severe itching, skin infections, and loss of hair. You can control external parasites with insecticides that you use both on the animal and on the environment—many of these pests live part of their life off the dog in the grass of your lawn or in convenient nooks and crannies in your home. The medication you use will depend on the type of parasite you're dealing with, and your veterinarian can identify the problem and suggest a suitable insecticide.

The most common internal parasites live in the dog's intestines, and if they're left untreated they can cause serious problems like chronic diarrhea, anemia (red blood cell deficiency), poor condition of coat, and cough. Some internal parasites attack other organs, like the heart. All dogs are susceptible to internal parasites.

Unlike some external parasites, which you may (after some experience of dog ownership) be able to identify and treat yourself with a topical product such as a flea powder, internal parasites always require professional veterinary attention. Although you should be able to recognize the signs of a possible problem, you should never try to diagnose or treat internal parasites yourself. Your veterinarian will make the diagnosis by examining a sample of the dog's feces under a microscope—in most cases he's looking not for the parasite itself but for the minute eggs that the organism deposits in the stool. Once the diagnosis is made, the veterinarian will prescribe the appropriate medication. Don't ever medicate for internal parasites without professional advice—worming medicines are poisons and should not be administered at random.

The internal parasites that most commonly infect the dog's intestines are roundworms, hookworms, whipworms, tapeworms, giardia, and coccidia. The potentially very dangerous heartworm affects the dog's heart.

The following discussion of individual parasites will help you recognize the signs of parasitic infestation.

EXTERNAL PARASITES

FLEAS

Fleas are tiny brown insects that live on the dog's skin and feed by sucking the animal's blood. If you part the dog's fur you can see them moving. Fleas can't fly, but they can jump quite a distance and travel easily from one dog to another. They irritate the skin and make the dog scratch—although not all scratching dogs have fleas. And the saliva of the flea is a potent allergen that can set up a severe allergic reaction in a susceptible dog. In such a case the dog will lose a great deal of hair, especially above the tail, and develop scaly skin on his back. He will probably scratch himself so persistently that the skin bleeds. This condition is known as flea-bite dermatitis.

Besides irritating the skin, the flea is the intermediate host of the tapeworm—an internal parasite which is described later in this chapter.

In some parts of the United States, fleas are a year-round problem. In the Northern climates the winter cold will kill fleas outdoors; they can, however, winter over comfortably in your home.

Life cycle.   The adult flea lays its eggs on the dog or in the environment—on the lawn, in the dog's bed, in your carpet. The eggs laid on the dog fall off and, after a period that varies from three to five days depending on environmental temperature and humidity, hatch into legless larvae—the immature form of the insect. After feeding for four to eight days on the ground, the larvae spin cocoons in which they remain for five days to five weeks. Again, the length of time depends on environmental conditions. The adult fleas emerge from the cocoons and hop on to the dog. The female fleas reproduce almost immediately, and the cycle starts again.

Signs and diagnosis.   The most common indication that a dog has fleas is extreme itching. But don't assume that the itching is caused by fleas unless you actually see them. Spread the dog's fur on the rump or in the groin and look for the adult fleas running through the fur. Another way to check is to rub the animal's rump vigorously on to a wet white paper towel. Flea feces are mostly blood, and any black specks that fall on the towel and smear to a reddish-brown color are evidence of flea infestation. As mentioned earlier, an allergic reaction to prolonged exposure to the fleas' saliva may cause hair loss, scaliness on the back, and raw patches where the dog has scratched himself. It's to be hoped that you can get rid of the fleas before this happens.

Control and treatment. Control of fleas can be a wearisome business and you'll need the advice of your veterinarian and, possibly, an exterminator. You must treat the affected dog and all the other animals in the household, and you must also treat the animals' indoor and, in some cases, outdoor environment. If the dog has scratched himself raw, cortisone given orally or by injection should clear up the condition.

A number of dog shampoos and dips are available and will effectively kill the fleas. Sprays and powders are quick and effective. Ask your veterinarian to recommend a product, and use it strictly according to the manufacturer's instructions. Remember that any insecticide you use on your pet can cause side effects like vomiting, excess salivation, or skin irritation. Check before you use the product that you know what to do if there are side effects. A flea collar can help keep the animal from becoming reinfested.

Once you've treated the animal or animals, thoroughly clean the house, the dog's kennel, and any other areas where the fleas may breed. Your veterinarian can recommend an insecticide, frequently a spray that will fog the infested area.

TICKS

Ticks are small, insect-like creatures that usually inhabit the parts of the dog where the hair is thin. They bury their heads in the skin and suck the animal's blood. Although they can be found anywhere on the body they seem to prefer the head area, especially around the ears. When they are swollen with blood, ticks are about the size of a pea. Usually, the only result of a tick bite is mild irritation. But there's one exception: certain ticks carry a potent neurotoxin—a poisonous substance that affects the nervous system—and their bite can cause profound weakness in a dog, sometimes resulting in total paralysis.

Life cycle. After gorging itself on the dog's blood, the female tick drops off and lays its eggs in a crack or crevice

indoors or outdoors, where they incubate and then hatch
into larvae or "seed ticks." These attach themselves to the
dog and feed on the blood, then fall to the ground and, after
a week or two, molt to their next stage of development—the
nymph stage. Again, they find the dog, feed, fall off, and
molt to the adult stage. The adult male and female ticks
mate, and the cycle repeats. If the whole cycle occurs in your
home, your dog will be continuously infected. If the cycle
occurs outside, your dog or any other dog that enters the
area can become infected. Your dog will also bring the ticks
into the house.

Signs and diagnosis. The signs of tick infection aren't
always as obvious as you might expect. The dog won't
usually scratch excessively, and unless you actually see and
remove them, the ticks can live a long and comfortable life.
The best way of keeping your animal clear of this parasite is
to check the skin regularly around the head, ears, and neck,
under the arms, and in any other thin-haired area.

     If the tick is of the type that carries a neurotoxin,
tick paralysis will develop. The neurotoxin in the tick's
saliva enters the dog's bloodstream and signs of paralysis
appear within 36 hours. The dog becomes progressively
weaker, and the paralysis spreads to the back legs, the front
legs, and then to the respiratory system.

Control and treatment. As with fleas, getting rid of ticks
involves treating both the dog and his surroundings. If there
are only a few ticks on the animal, remove them with
tweezers. Use the tweezers to grasp the tick where its head is
embedded in the skin, and pull the tick out. Destroy the tick
after removal. Try to remove the whole tick; if the head is left
embedded in the dog's skin it may cause a sore. Don't ever
use a cigarette to remove a tick fron the dog's skin; you'll
almost certainly burn the dog.

     If your dog is heavily infected, bathe him with an
insecticidal solution recommended by your veterinarian.
Put a tick collar on the dog and use sprays or powders
periodically, as directed by the veterinarian, to help keep the
dog free of further tick problems.

When you've treated the dog, treat the environment. You can use an insecticide to fog your home. Sprays are also available to use in your yard, on the doghouse, the lawn, woodpiles, or other areas where the ticks may be hiding. Ask your veterinarian where you should apply insecticide. In the case of a severe infestation, you may also need to get the advice of an exterminator.

In the case of tick paralysis, prompt treatment should lead to complete recovery within a matter of hours. Remove the ticks and take the dog immediately to the veterinarian, who will bathe the dog with an insecticide solution to destroy any ticks you have not already removed. As soon as the toxin ceases to enter the bloodstream, recovery begins. Untreated, however, tick paralysis is fatal.

LICE

Lice are tiny wingless insects, barely visible to the naked eye, that live their entire life cycle on the dog. There are a number of different types of lice, but each type is host-specific—that is, it can only live on one species of animal. Dog lice live only on dogs and can't survive on cats or humans; human lice don't infect animals. The lice pass from one host to another by direct contact, and can be found on all parts of the body.

Life cycle. The female lice lay eggs on the dog but, unlike the flea eggs which fall off the animal, these eggs (or nits) are attached to the hair shaft. They are small, white particles and look a bit like human dandruff. The parasite lives out its life and reproductive cycle on the dog.

Signs and diagnosis. The signs of infection are usually limited to itching. If the infestation is severe, the dog may scratch himself raw.

Control and treatment. It's important to have lice identified by your veterinarian, but once you know what you're dealing with treatment is straight forward and successful. Lice are easier to get rid of than some of the other external parasites. Because they live out their full cycle on the dog, it's only necessary to treat the animal. If there's more than one dog in the family, however, it is necessary to treat them all since they will certainly have passed the lice to one another.

Your veterinarian can recommend a dog shampoo, dip, or spray to get rid of the lice. You'll probably have to repeat the treatment at weekly intervals for three weeks. Read the label on the product carefully and follow instructions. If the dog has scratched himself raw, the veterinarian will prescribe medication to heal the lesions.

MANGE MITES

Mites are small, insect-like parasites that spend their whole life cycle on the dog and will live only a short time off the animal. They are very small and can't be seen without a microscope. Like lice, mange mites are host-specific. Most animal species are susceptible to some type of mange mite, but the types that affect dogs won't affect cats or people, and vice versa. Of the several types of mange mites that affect dogs, the most common are sarcoptic and demodectic mites.

Sarcoptic Mange Mites

Sarcoptic mange, commonly known as "scabies," is caused by a microscopic, round, four-legged mite. It's highly contagious between dogs.

Life cycle. The female mite tunnels into the skin and lays eggs which hatch in 10 to 14 days. The dog hosts the mites for their entire life cycle.

Signs and diagnosis. The signs of sarcoptic mange vary, but the most common are scaliness and loss of hair around the edges of the ears and on the elbows, chest, and back. Intense itching is a characteristic of this condition. Your veterinarian diagnoses sarcoptic mange by scraping a suspected lesion and examining it under a microscope for the presence of the mite or its eggs. Skin scrapings, however, do not always reveal the presence of the culprit and here it's possible that you may be able to help. If you have developed small marks similar to mosquito bites on your own body, the mange mite may be responsible. Although the mite cannot live on humans, it will bite.

Control and treatment. Your veterinarian will prescribe an insecticide to cure sarcoptic mange. You'll probably need to apply the medication weekly for three weeks to get rid of the mites completely, and all dogs in the household must be treated at the same time. Lime-sulphur dips and other miticides give good results. Long-haired dogs that are severely infected should be clipped before treatment. Your veterinarian can also prescribe medications to control itching and prevent further skin infection.

Demodectic Mange

This type of mange is often called "red mange" and is caused by a microscopic mite that has an elongated shape and lives deep in the skin in hair follicles. Demodectic mange can be localized to one or two areas of the dog's body or generalized over the whole body. A curious property of this parasite is that you may never know the dog has got it because the animal's defense mechanisms keep it under control. Perhaps 50 or 60 percent of all dogs have the infection but show no signs of it, and a perfectly normal bitch who has never shown any signs of demodectic mange can be a carrier and infect all her pups.

Life cycle. The only way demodectic mange mites can be transferred is from the mother to the puppy at birth. The mites live dormant in the skin until the puppy is about four months old, at which point they become active and the puppy usually begins to show signs of hair loss, particularly around the muzzle, eyes, and forelimbs.

Signs and diagnosis. As mentioned above, hair loss is the first indicator of demodectic mange. In severe cases, secondary bacterial infections can cause the skin to become thickened and inflamed. Sometimes, but not always, the dog will scratch to relieve itching caused by the condition. Your veterinarian can diagnose the demodectic mange only from microscopic examination of skin scrapings from a suspected area.

Control and treatment. Many insecticidal preparations have been put forward as cures for demodectic mange, but in fact, treatment has until recently proved very disappointing. Localized lesions often respond well to treatment, but generalized demodectic mange has always been very frustrating to the owner and the veterinarian. Since recovery depends on the body's own defense mechanism, the dog must be in top shape for the defense mechanism (antibodies) to work properly. This means that the dog must be well fed, free of any other parasites, and not under undue stress. Antibiotics are used to control secondary infection. Recently a new drug, amitraz, has become available and has proven very effective in eliminating the demodectic mange mite. Amitraz is available only through your veterinarian and has proven 99 percent effective in curing this once dreaded parasitic disease.

EAR MITES

Ear mites, often called "ear mange," are insect-like creatures that resemble the sarcoptic mange mite. They live in the ear canal—hence the name—and can barely be seen with the naked eye.

Life cycle. The ear mite lives its whole life in the ear canal. Occasionally a few travel to other parts of the body, but these wanderers don't seem to cause any problems. The mite is host-specific and is highly contagious between animals of the same species.

Signs and diagnosis. Several clues can warn you that your dog has ear mites. Head-shaking and intense itching are often the first signs (but these signs can also indicate ear problems other than mites). Often there's a brown, waxy material in the ears, and if a secondary infection has set in the ear canal will emit an unpleasant odor.

Control and treatment. Ear mites respond well to treatment, and in many cases you won't even need to see the veterinarian. Thorough daily cleaning of the ears with cotton swabs is a must (the grooming section tells you how to do it), and often plain mineral oil dropped in the ears after every cleaning is enough to kill the mites. This daily cleaning should be continued for 10 to 14 days. However, if the dog is still obviously distressed after a few days, see a veterinarian. If home treatment doesn't work, your veterinarian will prescribe medication. If one dog in the household has ear mites, you must treat all the animals in the house at the same time, even if their ears don't seem to be infected, and repeat the treatment daily for 10 to 14 days to make sure that all the mites are dead.

If the smell of the ears indicates that a secondary infection has set in, your veterinarian will prescribe an antibiotic ointment. Remember that any time home treatment does not seem to work within three to four days, you should consult the veterinarian.

INTERNAL PARASITES

ROUNDWORMS

These are long, white worms that look like spaghetti, and they're easy to recognize in the dog's stool or vomit. It's probably safe to assume that most puppies will contract roundworms from their mother, but older dogs usually become resistant to them. Under normal sanitary conditions these parasites are not such a serious problem as other, faster-developing parasites.

Life cycle. The most common method of infection is through the uterus of the mother dog. Scientists have learned that the dormant, microscopic larvae present in the mother become active when she's about 42 days pregnant. The larvae (immature roundworms) migrate from the mother's tissues to those of the puppies while they are still in the uterus. After the pup is born, the larvae either develop into adult worms in the pup's intestine, or remain dormant in the tissues and become active when the puppy is older. In the case of a female, these dormant larvae will become active during her pregnancy and, in turn, infect her puppies. Another method of infection is through the mother's milk. The larvae pass to the puppy through the milk and develop in the same way as those passed before birth.

Roundworm infections aren't limited to puppies. Older dogs can develop roundworms from contact with stools passed by an infected dog. However, older dogs usually become resistant to roundworms and commonly pass them out either in the stool or in vomit.

Signs and diagnosis. Puppies heavily infected with roundworms are thin and usually have diarrhea. Sometimes they look pot-bellied, but this by itself isn't sufficient proof of infection. Often you'll know for sure because the puppy passes the spaghetti-like worms in the stool, or vomits them up. Your veterinarian makes the diagnosis by analyzing the stool.

Control and treatment. The best method of control is to have stool samples checked periodically. If there's a problem, remove the infected stool immediately after the dog defecates in order to avoid reinfection, and worm the dog according to your veterinarian's recommendation. Contrary to what some people think, it's *not* necessary to worm a dog monthly to control roundworms. Over-medication can cause serious problems like vomiting and diarrhea, so medicate only on the advice of your veterinarian.

HOOKWORMS

Hookworms are small parasites (less than half an inch long) that affect dogs of all ages, although young puppies seem to be more severely affected than older dogs. The parasites live in the small intestine and attach themselves to the lining of the intestine. Hookworms are blood-suckers, and if there are enough of them, they can cause severe anemia (a deficiency of red blood cells) and even death.

Life cycle. Under ideal hot and humid conditions, hookworm eggs passed in the stool of an infected dog incubate very quickly—within 24 hours—to the immature larva stage at which they become active and can infect any dog that comes in contact with them. All the dog has to do to become infected is walk on the soil where the eggs or larvae are present. The larvae can penetrate the skin directly or the eggs can enter the dog's system when he licks them off his feet and swallows them.

Signs and diagnosis. As mentioned earlier, young puppies are particularly affected by hookworms. Young animals that are infected look very thin, and their fur is scruffy and dull. Diarrhea tinged with blood is common in both young and older dogs. The veterinarian diagnoses hookworms by microscopic examination of the stool.

Control and treatment Hookworm infestation is treated with medications specifically indicated for this parasite. Your veterinarian will set up a worming routine for your dog, and just as important as the medication is environmental clean-up. Your dog will become reinfected time and again, no matter how often you worm him, if the ground where he walks remains infected. And remember that he can reinfect himself from his own stools, so they must be removed promptly. You can get yard sprays to kill the hookworm eggs, but continuing attention to sanitation is of the utmost importance. Having your veterinarian check stool samples regularly (frequency depends on the climate in your area) is the most practical method of controlling hookworms.

WHIPWORMS

Whipworms affect dogs of all ages and live in the dog's cecum—the short, closed end sac of the lower intestinal tract. The whipworm is very small and can rarely be seen with the naked eye, and it gets the name from the shape of its body: the top half is long and thin and the back part is short and thick.

Life cycle. A dog becomes infested with whipworms by walking on contaminated ground soil and then licking the eggs from his feet. The whipworm eggs are thick walled and very hard to destroy, so they can stay in the soil for long periods. In northern climates they winter over and become a severe problem when the soil begins to thaw in the spring. The ingested eggs develop into adult worms in the dog's intestine, lay eggs which are passed in the stool, and so continue the cycle.

Signs and diagnosis. The most significant effect of whipworm infection is inflammation of the bowel which causes intermittent bouts of diarrhea. If your dog has been having diarrhea off and on and you've ruled out other possible causes, it's possible that he's got whipworms.

Control and treatment. Your veterinarian will diagnose whipworms from a microscopic examination of the stool, and can choose from a number of remedies for treating them. However, because poor sanitation is a frequent cause of whipworm infestation, environmental control is as important as medication. Reinfestation is a frequent problem and you may find that you have to worm your dog, on your veterinarian's recommendation, several times a year. Try to forestall problems by having your veterinarian check stool samples regularly (frequency depends on the climate in your area), keep your yard clean, and keep your dog away from areas where you know owners don't clean up after their dogs.

TAPEWORMS

Tapeworms are flat and, traditionally, got their name from their shape and their resemblance to pieces of tape. In fact, tapeworm segments passed in the dog's stool look like grains of rice. It's possible to see them moving as they are passed. Each segment is an egg packet containing a large number of eggs.

Life cycle. Unlike roundworms, hookworms, and whipworms, tapeworms are not transmitted directly from the stool. Tapeworm infection occurs when the dog eats an infected intermediate host—in this country the flea is most likely to be the culprit. The flea has already fed on the tapeworm eggs contained in the segments passed in the stool of an infected animal. Inside the flea, the eggs mature to the stage at which they can infect a dog. The flea lives in the dogs's fur and, in the process of grooming himself, the dog swallows the flea. As the flea is digested the eggs are released in the dog's intestine and grow to adult size. These adult tapeworms, in turn, lay eggs contained in segments which are passed in the dog's stool, and the cycle starts over. Mice, rabbits, and fish can also act as intermediate hosts for the tapeworm. So can cattle and pigs, and a dog that eats raw meat from any of these hosts can become infected.

Signs and diagnosis. Tapeworms seldom cause much real trouble beyond mild diarrhea and some rectal itching. You're most likely to spot them by examining the hair around the rectum for the rice-like segments that contain the tapeworm eggs.

Control and treatment.   As with so many parasite problems, treating tapeworms is a two-part task—you have to rid the dog of tapeworms and rid the environment of the intermediate host. Your veterinarian can treat the dog for tapeworms with an oral or injected medication. If the dog is getting the tapeworms from fleas, however, you won't make any progress unless you get rid of the fleas, too. The section on external parasites tells you how.

COCCIDIA

Unlike the intestinal parasites discussed so far, this parasite is not a worm. It's a one-celled organism (protozoan) that lives in the intestine and usually causes problems in very young puppies. You can only see it under a microscope.

Life cycle.   Coccidia multiply rapidly in the lining of the intestines and are transferred from one animal to another in the stool.

Signs and diagnosis.   Very young puppies are usually most susceptible to coccidia, and this parasite is often found in puppies that have been housed with a lot of companions in unsanitary conditions. Typical warning signs are emaciated appearance and diarrhea which sometimes contains blood. Very often, secondary infections cause discharge from the eyes or nose.

Control and treatment.   If it's not severe, coccidia infection is self-limiting and disappears when the surroundings are returned to a sanitary condition. However, medications are available, and your veterinarian can prescribe medication for the dog and make suggestions for maintaining a clean environment.

GIARDIA

Giardia parasites are similar to coccidia in that they are also one-celled organisms or protozoa. Giardia, however, can move around by means of a hair-like structure called the flagellum.

Life cycle.   This parasite lives in the intestines and is transferred in the stool. Its life cycle is perpetuated by unsanitary conditions. It seems to be triggered to activity by stress, and the "cyst" or nonactive form of giardia can be carried by dogs with no apparent ill effects. When the dog is under stress, however—for instance, when the animal gets ill or moves to a strange environment—the parasites become active and the dog begins to show signs of infection.

Signs and diagnosis.   Puppies that are housed with other puppies in unsanitary conditions are very susceptible to this parasite—in fact, it's a grossly overlooked disease among puppies. The most common sign of trouble is diarrhea that contains blood or mucus. Any puppy that has diarrhea that won't clear up with conventional treatment may be infested with giardia.

The veterinarian diagnoses giardia from a stool sample, but the method of examination is different from that used for other internal parasites. In this case the veterinarian does a direct fecal smear, which involves taking a very fresh stool sample—not more than 15 to 20 minutes old—and examining a drop of it for the moving parasite.

Control and treatment.   Medications can clear up giardia very quickly, but as with other parasites it's equally important to improve the cleanliness of the environment.

HEARTWORM

Heartworm disease is caused by a nematode (worm) that lives in its adult stage in the right side of the dog's heart. Heartworms are transmitted from one dog to another by mosquitoes, and do all their damage in the adult stage by which time the worms can be up to 12 inches long. Because the infection is transmitted by mosquitoes, heartworm disease used to be a real problem only in the warm, southern coastal areas of the United States. Increased mobility of the population (and its dogs) has caused the disease to spread widely and it is becoming a very serious threat to dogs in most areas of the country.

Life cycle.   There are three stages in the life cycle of the heartworm. 1. The adult female worm lays live immature worms in the infected dog's bloodstream. 2. These immature worms can only develop further in the mosquito, so they remain in the dog's bloodstream until the animal is bitten by a mosquito. They then develop inside the mosquito to the infective larva stage; this process takes about two weeks. 3. The infected mosquito bites an uninfected dog, and passes the infective larvae into the dog's bloodstream. The larvae live in the dog for about three months and then migrate to the dog's heart and settle in the right ventricle of the heart and the adjoining blood vessels. Within another three months the worms are fully grown; they begin to reproduce, and the cycle starts over.

Signs and diagnosis.   Severe infection of adult heartworms causes cough, breathing difficulties, fatigue, and general weakness. As the disease progresses, the dog's heart, liver, and lungs become severely damaged. Visible symptoms of the disease do not appear until the advanced stages, so it's important to have the dog checked regularly in order to arrest the disease in the early stages.

Control and treatment.   Prevention of heartworm disease is better than cure—in fact, if the disease has reached an advanced stage before it is diagnosed, cure may be impossible. Your dog should be checked regularly for heartworms at intervals that your veterinarian will recommend according to where you live. Preventive medication is available and should be given daily throughout the mosquito season.

If the blood test administered by the veterinarian reveals the presence of heartworms, medications are prescribed. It may require several treatments with different medications to clear the dog of both the adult and immature worms. Once this treatment is completed, the dog should be given daily medication to prevent further infection. This preventive medication, however, can be given only to dogs that are free of established heartworm infection; in an infected dog it can cause a severe or fatal reaction.

HOME AND EMERGENCY CARE

Sound nutrition, regular exercise and grooming, routine visits to the veterinarian, and lots of affection on your part are all part of your basic plan for your dog's well-being. As a responsible owner you also need to know how to administer some home health care—like how to take your dog's temperature and how to give medication—and what to do in an emergency. This preparedness goes from having around the house the supplies you might need to administer simple first aid, to knowing how to restrain an injured animal and get him to the veterinarian, to mastering the techniques of artificial respiration and cardiopulmonary resuscitation (CPR).

This chapter supplies just such important information. The chart on page 127 tells you just what a well-equipped dog owner needs in the way of first aid supplies—and why. Then there's specific how-to information on taking a dog's temperature and administering liquid medication and pills (not always an easy matter if the dog doesn't want to cooperate).

This is followed by a section that discusses how to restrain, transport, and administer emergency life-support care to an injured dog, and then covers (in alphabetical order) major emergency situations such as burns, choking, drowning, poisoning, and shock.

TAKING A DOG'S TEMPERATURE

Just as with humans, a rise in a dog's body temperature indicates a problem, and a thermometer is an essential part of your home care kit. A thermometer with a thick bulb end is best. To use it, shake the thermometer down until it reads below 96° F/36° C and cover it halfway with petroleum or IC-Y jelly; hold the dog's tail upright, gently insert the thermometer into his rectum, and hold it there for at least three minutes. Then remove the thermometer, wipe off the jelly with a tissue, and take the reading. A dog's

Taking your dog's temperature gives you an important clue to the state of his health.

normal body temperature is 100° to 103°F/38°C (an average of 101.5°F)—considerably higher than that of a human. An elevated temperature in a dog is anything over 103°F/39°C, and can indicate a number of conditions—some serious, some not—ranging from simple excitement or over-exertion to infection.

ADMINISTERING ORAL MEDICATION

Many dogs, especially the more trusting characters, accept medication by mouth without too much trouble. Independent or suspicious types get insulted at the very idea and may give you a hard time, so it helps to have someone restrain the dog while you give the medication. In this case, have your assistant pass one arm under the dog's neck, holding the dog's throat gently in the crook of the arm so that the animal can breathe easily. Then the assistant should pass the other arm over or under the dog's middle, using gentle but firm pressure to hold the body steady. If the dog is really uncooperative, tie his mouth loosely with a strip of cloth or gauze so that he can open his jaw only slightly (the illustrations on page 105 show how to do this). This only works if you're giving liquid medication. If you're giving pills you have to be able to open the dog's mouth.

Liquids. If you're giving a liquid medication, gently tip the dog's head back a little and pull out the lower lip at the corner to make a pouch. Using a plastic eye dropper or dosage syringe, place the medication into the pouch a little at a time, allowing each small amount to be swallowed before you give any more. Rub the dog's throat gently to stimulate swallowing.

Pills. To give a dog a pill, grasp his upper jaw with one hand over muzzle, then press the lips over the upper teeth by pressing your thumb on one side and your fingers on the other so that the dog's lips are between his teeth and your fingers. Firm pressure will force the mouth open. Hold the

Giving liquid medications.

Giving medication in pill form.

When you need to give your dog medication by mouth, make it easy on both of you by following these illustrations and instructions.

pill between the thumb and index finger of your free hand and place the pill as far back as possible in the dog's mouth. Then close the dog's mouth and fold your hand round the muzzle to keep the mouth closed, and with your free hand gently rub the dog's throat to stimulate swallowing.

THE RIGHT WAY TO HELP AN INJURED DOG

RESTRAINING AN INJURED DOG

If the dog is conscious, you must get close enough to him to look him over carefully. Your goal is to ease the dog's suffering and stabilize his vital signs quickly before transporting him to a veterinarian. An injured dog is usually frightened and in pain, and unless he feels very secure with your presence, he may try to escape or to bite you. Therefore, approach the dog slowly, talking in a reassuring tone of voice as you do so; then stoop down to the dog's level to make him even more comfortable with your presence.

You can tell a great deal about how the dog will react to you by observing the eyes and facial expression. If the dog is very submissive, he will show this by having the head slightly lowered, and the mouth drawn back a little into what appears to be a smile. Occasionally a very submissive dog will even roll over on his back with the hind legs spread apart. This animal is usually easy to handle, but continue to use caution.

First, slowly attempt to pet the dog under the jaw. If this is accepted, then pet the top of his head. Continue to talk reassuringly. It is best not to take chances, so slip a length of rope around the animal's neck, and then apply a muzzle. At this point, you can examine him thoroughly, and then treat the injuries.

If the dog is growling and his eyes are dilated, do not attempt to touch him. Continue to talk reassuringly, but try to slip a rope over the dog's head and around his neck.

Then muzzle the dog before you try to assess the extent of his injuries.

TRANSPORTING AN INJURED DOG

Try not to move an injured dog more than necessary, and get him to a veterinarian as soon as possible. Have someone call the veterinarian to be certain he is prepared for your animal.

Depending on the injury, wrap the dog in blankets or use a blanket or flat board as a stretcher. If you suspect a broken back use a stiff board and tie the dog to it with strips of cloth. Make sure the board will fit into your car, then move the board next to the dog, put the ties underneath the board, and gently lift or slide the dog onto it. Fasten the ties over the dog to eliminate as much movement as possible.

If the dog is not breathing and/or his heart is not beating, the dog will probably die or may be dead already. Begin cardiopulmonary resuscitation as detailed below. CPR should be continued on the way to the veterinarian. Keep trying, and don't give up on the CPR too easily.

CARDIOPULMONARY RESUSCITATION (CPR)

If the dog's heart is not beating and the dog is not breathing, proceed as follows:

If the dog weighs up to 45 pounds:

1. Turn the dog on his back.

2. Kneel down at the dog's head.

3. Clasp your hands over the dog's chest with your palms resting on either side of his chest.

4. Compress your palms on the chest firmly for a count of "2" and release for a count of "1." Use moderate pressure, and repeat about 30 times in 30 seconds.

If the dog weighs more than 45 pounds:

1. Turn the dog on his side.

2. Place the palm of your hand in the middle of the dog's chest.

3. Press for a count of "2"; release for a count of "1."

4. Use firm pressure, and repeat about 30 times in 30 seconds.

The following procedures apply to dogs of all sizes:

1. Alternately (after 30 seconds): Hold the dog's mouth and lips closed and blow firmly into the nostrils. Blow for 3 seconds, take a deep breath, and repeat until you feel resistance or see the chest rise. Try to repeat this 20 times in 60 seconds.

2. After one minute, stop. Watch the chest for movement to indicate that the dog is breathing and feel for the heartbeat by placing your fingers about 2" behind the dog's elbow in the center of the chest. If the dog is still not breathing, and the heart is not beating, continue CPR. Continue CPR on the way to the veterinarian and don't give up.

If you are successful in reviving the dog, take him as soon as possible to the veterinarian for examination. The veterinarian will assess the extent of the animal's injuries and advise on after-care.

EMERGENCIES: WHAT TO EXPECT AND WHAT TO DO

ANIMAL BITE

When a dog gets into a fight with another dog, a cat, or a wild animal, damage can occur to both the skin and the underlying tissue. Many dog fights can be avoided by not permitting your dog to run loose and by keeping him on a leash when you walk him. The dog should also be trained to obey your commands.

If your dog does get into a fight, do not try to break it up with your bare hands. A fighting dog will bite anything in his way, including you. Pull your leashed dog out of harm's way or use a long stick to separate the combatants.

When the fight is over, examine your dog carefully for hidden wounds. You'll often find punctures around the neck area and on the legs. Look through the hair carefully to find blood stains which indicate that the skin has been punctured.

Clip the hair from around the wound to assess the damage, then flush with 3% hydrogen peroxide to prevent infection—one of the major complications of a bite.

The dog should then be seen by a veterinarian. Although there may be only a few punctures, extensive damage may have been done to underlying muscles through the pressure of the bite. And if the wounds are deep enough to require stitches, they should be treated professionally as soon as possible.

Unless there is extensive bleeding, bite wounds should be left open to drain until the dog is seen by the veterinarian. When tissue is damaged, fluid accumulates in the area and if the wound is not left open to drain, a painful swelling occurs and the site becomes a perfect medium for the growth of bacteria and infection.

A dog can develop tetanus from a bite, although

this happens rarely. The veterinarian will decide whether a tetanus shot is necessary.

If the animal responsible for the bites is a domestic pet, try to find out if it has been innoculated against rabies. If the biter is a wild animal such as a skunk or raccoon, efforts should be made to destroy it or confine it so that it can be destroyed and the brain examined for rabies. Never touch the animal with your bare hands, even if it has been killed. Wear gloves or wrap the body in a blanket. Your veterinarian will take care of the rabies examination.

BLEEDING

With a bleeding injury, the main purpose of first aid is to prevent excessive blood loss which can lead to shock. Pressure is applied to the wound, usually with a bandage or similar dressing to allow the normal clotting mechanism of the blood to stop the leak. Clotting is a complex process, but basically, the blood cells form a fine screen over the wound and thus prevent further loss of blood. It is important not to remove the dressing once it has been applied. If you lift it to look at the wound, you will break up the clots that are forming and the wound will continue to bleed.

If the wound continues to bleed through the dressing, it will be necessary to use a tourniquet.

To apply a tourniquet, follow this procedure:

1. Fold a tie, belt, or piece of cloth to about an inch in width; do *not* use rope, wire, or string. Place the material between the wound and the heart, an inch or two above the wound but not touching it.

2. Tie a stick or ruler to the material with a single knot.

3. Twist the stick until the bleeding stops, but no tighter.

4. Wrap a piece of cloth around the stick and the animal to keep the tourniquet in place.

Then take the dog to the veterinarian. If it's a long journey to the veterinarian, loosen the tourniquet for one to two minutes every 15 minutes.

The tourniquet should be used only as a last resort, because it not only stops the bleeding, it also prevents blood from getting to other tissues in the area, which become oxygen-starved and die.

Blood is carried away from the heart by the arteries and returned by the veins. If an artery is cut the blood will spurt with each beat of the heart. Cut arteries require immediate care to stop the bleeding and usually require veterinary repair.

The paws and legs of a dog are vulnerable to injury from broken glass, nails, etc. The multiple blood vessels are close to the skin surface and are easily cut when the skin is injured, which is why the paws and legs bleed so heavily when injured. An injured ear will also bleed heavily because the skin over the ear is so thin. Firm bandaging of these areas is required to control the bleeding.

BROKEN BONES

With dogs, as with human beings, all bones are subject to breakage, but leg fractures are by far the most common. It is important to remember that dogs have a high pain tolerance and often a dangling leg seems to cause no pain. Therefore, don't be afraid to handle the fractured limb as long as you do it gently. The dog will let you know if it hurts. If the dog is in pain or if the fracture is open, do not attempt to apply a splint. Simply clean the wound, then hold a large towel under the limb for support and take the dog to a veterinarian.

An open fracture is one where the bone is protruding or there is a break in the skin over the broken bone.

First aid efforts should be directed to the control of infection, since the exposed bone is subject to bacterial invasion. Proper cleaning is vital, but use only 3% hydrogen peroxide to clean the wound because antiseptics may cause tissue damage.

A closed fracture is one where the bone is broken but the skin intact. The leg should be splinted by tying it to a stick or a rolled magazine or newspaper. Do not confuse splinting with setting the limb, which should be done by a professional. Splinting is only a temporary procedure, so you may use any firm material at hand. The purpose of a splint is to prevent further damage by immobilizing the limb and to make the animal more comfortable during the trip to the veterinarian.

BURNS

Burns can be caused by fire, heat, boiling liquids, chemicals, and electricity. All are painful and can cause damage, even death.

Superficial burns, evidenced by pain and reddening of the skin, are usually not serious. However, first aid should be given as soon as possible to ease the pain. Burns tend to "cook" the skin, and in order to stop this cooking process, cold water or ice packs should be applied to the burned area at once.

Never apply butter or grease to a burn. At one time this was the recommended treatment, but it is now known that these substances can actually make the wound worse.

Third degree burns are far more serious and depending on how much of the body is involved they can cause death. The deeper the layers of skin involved, the more likely the dog is to go into shock. The outer skin layers are destroyed and the unprotected lower layers are then susceptible to infection. If the burns are extensive, a great deal of fluid from the tissue cells is lost, and shock is inevitable. Therefore, treatment for shock (as described later in this section) is your first priority and should be continued until professional help can be obtained.

Chemical burns can also endanger pets. Such products as drain cleaner or paint thinner can cause serious skin damage, and poisoning if ingested.

If you notice a chemical odor on your dog, often the first sign of this type of burn, bathe him immediately. Use mild soap and lather well; rinse thoroughly until the chemical odor has disappeared. Do not use solvents of any kind on the skin.

Unlike heat burns, a soothing antibiotic can then be applied to a chemical burn until the dog can be treated by a veterinarian. Be sure all the chemical is removed before the ointment is applied.

Electrical burns are most often caused by chewing on an electrical cord. The burns are almost always located on both sides of the mouth or lips. Most of these burns are minor and will heal well if kept clean with 3% hydrogen peroxide. Chewing an electric cord can also cause shock, which is discussed later in this section.

Take the following precautions to avoid your dog becoming accidentally burned:

- In the kitchen, where the dog is often underfoot while you're cooking in hopes of a handout, be especially careful while handling hot water or cooking oil.
- Keep all chemicals—paint thinner or drain cleaner, for example—where your pets cannot get at them.
- Keep electrical cords concealed or coiled when possible, and do not leave a puppy (or any inquisitive dog) alone where cords are within its reach.

CHOKING

When a dog is choking on a foreign object, he needs help at once. The harder he tries to breathe, the more panicky he becomes. Your goal is to open the airway without being bitten. If you cannot reach the obstruction with your fingers, (or if the dog is struggling too much to let you try) turn the dog upside down and shake him. This will often dislodge the object and propel it out of the mouth.

You cannot, of course, turn a German Shepherd or a Great Dane upside down and shake him, so with a larger dog you should employ the abdominal compression technique, which can be compared to pushing the air out of a beach ball. To do this, place the dog on his side on the floor, place your hand just behind the rib cage, press down and slightly forward quickly and firmly, then release. Repeat rapidly several times until the object is expelled. The sudden thrusts on the abdomen cause the diaphragm to bulge forward into the chest. This in turn forces air, and frequently the object, out of the windpipe. If the object is not expelled, the dog must have immediate professional care.

If the dog is unconscious and you believe a foreign object is present, you must open the airway before giving artificial respiration or cardiac massage. If the dog cannot breathe, efforts to revive it will be fruitless.

The method of artificial respiration that is most effective includes blowing directly into the dog's nostrils. This inflates the lungs to the fullest and the result is maximum oxygenation.

Cardiac massage keeps the blood pumping through the vessels and stimulates the heart muscle to contract and start beating again. With smaller dogs, you compress the heart by actually squeezing it between your hands. This keeps the blood pressure up and starts normal heart muscle contractions.

The same results are achieved with larger dogs by a different method. The chest is usually too large to compress effectively between your hands, so only one hand is used, and the chest is compressed against the floor.

The purpose of artificial respiration and cardiac massage is to keep oxygenated blood circulating to the brain. If the brain does not receive this oxygenated blood, the dog will die.

CPR (cardiopulmonary resuscitation) is a combination of artificial respiration and cardiac massage and is described earlier in this section. It should be continued until the dog is breathing well or until you can get him to a veterinarian.

CONSTIPATION

Constipation—difficulty in moving the bowels and the production of hard, dry stools or no stool at all—is usually the result of faulty diet. It can be regulated by removing the offending substances from the diet (bones, for example) and feeding a balanced diet.

In some cases, however, a dog strains as though constipated but produces a soft stool; this is not constipation but a form of diarrhea. Sometimes this straining has nothing to do with diet, but is the result of a condition such as prostate enlargement, tumor of the colon, or perianal hernia. Because there are so many possible causes, do not attempt to treat the constipated dog with mineral oil, Milk of Magnesia, or any other home remedy without consulting the veterinarian.

DIARRHEA

Diarrhea—very loose stools—occurs when food is passed too rapidly through the intestines. It can be caused by food allergies, milk, spoiled food, or the presence of internal parasites. In some cases, diarrhea can be treated without a veterinarian's advice, but this is not always advisable because diarrhea can have much more serious causes such as tumors, viral infections, or diseases of the liver, kidney, or pancreas. Even if the cause of the diarrhea is not a matter of major concern, severe and continued diarrhea from any cause can result in dehydration.

If your dog has diarrhea but you do not consider it serious enough to call the veterinarian, institute home treatment by withholding food for 12 hours. Keep water available, however, to lessen the risk of dehydration. Kaopectate can be beneficial because it coats the irritated surfaces of the intestine. Give it every four to six hours at the rate of one teaspoonful per 10 to 15 pounds of the dog's weight.

If home treatment is not effective within 24 hours, call the veterinarian.

DROWNING

Dogs are naturally good swimmers for short distances, but they can get into trouble. Sometimes they get too far from the shore and tire trying to swim back, or fall into a swimming pool and cannot get up the steep sides.

Always protect yourself when trying to rescue a drowning dog. An extra few moments of preparation can save two lives, yours and the dog's. Throw a life preserver for the dog to catch onto with his teeth or try to hook his collar with a pole. If you must swim to the dog, bring a life preserver for the dog to hold on to. Once the dog is on land, you must first get the water out of his lungs. Failure to do this will certainly lead to death. Smaller dogs can simply be lifted by the hind legs, turned upside down, and shaken vigorously. A larger dog should be placed on a sloping surface with the head low and the body elevated to facilitate lung drainage.

When the lungs have been cleared, and if the dog is unconscious, it is important to check for heartbeat and breathing. If necessary, perform cardiopulmonary resuscitation (CPR). Many dogs that are seemingly dead can be revived with CPR, but if the water has not first been drained from the lungs, your efforts will be useless.

ELECTRICAL SHOCK

Grown dogs are seldom victims of electrical shocks. But puppies are naturally curious and will chew almost anything, including electrical cords. If the cord's insulation is punctured and the dog's mouth comes in contact with both wires, the dog will receive a shock and may be unable to release the cord.

Disconnect the cord from the socket immediately, before touching the dog. This is most important. If you touch the dog before disconnecting the cord, you could be electrocuted.

Once the cord is disconnected, you can safely touch the dog. Examine him carefully. Electrocution can cause severe heart damage and fluid accumulation in the lungs. Strong shock can stop the heart, and cardiopulmonary resuscitation (CPR) must be performed immediately to start the heart beating again.

Often the mouth will be burned from contact with the bare wires. These burns look much more serious than they are and will heal satisfactorily if cleaned and treated properly.

Most electrical shocks require professional attention and the victim should be taken to the veterinarian immediately.

FROSTBITE

When a dog is exposed to freezing temperatures for a long period of time, there is always the possibility of frostbite. The areas most likely to be frostbitten are those that have little or no hair such as the ears and tail tip, since there is minimum protection and a limited blood supply.

The affected areas should be warmed with moist heat, which will help to restore circulation. Use towels soaked in warm but not hot water—about 75°F/24°C is fine. Do not apply any kind of ointment to the frostbitten areas. Frequently the skin may turn very dark, which means the tissue is dead. If this happens, see a veterinarian for further treatment.

HEATSTROKE

Heatstroke occurs when the environment is so hot that the dog's body cannot maintain its normal temperature. Heatstroke is often caused by keeping a dog in a locked car parked in the sun, or by keeping him in any hot area without adequate ventilation.

Prompt treatment is urgent. The dog's body temperature can get as high as 107° F/41.5° C, and without quick cooling, severe brain damage and death will occur.

Your first goal is to cool the body by immersing the dog in a cold water bath or running a garden hose on the body; either treatment should be continued for at least 30 minutes. Then apply ice packs to the head and keep them in place while you transport the animal to a veterinarian.

Heatstroke can be prevented by making sure your dog has plenty of shade and ventilation. If you must take your dog driving with you in hot weather, park in the shade and leave all the windows partially open.

HYPOTHERMIA

Exposure to either cold water or freezing temperatures can cause hypothermia, an abnormal drop in body temperature. Survival will depend on how low the body temperature drops. A dog's normal body temperature is 100°-103° F/38° C. If it drops below 90° F/38° C for any length of time, normal bodily functions will be severely impaired.

First aid treatment at home requires getting the dog warm again with blankets and hot water bottles or a heating pad. Hypothermia always requires veterinary attention as soon as initial efforts to warm the dog have been made.

INSECT STING OR SPIDER BITE

If the dog is stung by a bee, wasp, yellow jacket, or hornet, the area quickly becomes swollen and painful. The raised area is called a wheal, and if the dog has been stung more than once, you will see several of these. The most serious implication of an insect bite or sting is a possible allergic reaction to the venom deposited by the insect.

If you see a wheal, apply ice to the area to reduce swelling and ease the pain. If a bee stung the dog, try to scrape the stinger off with a credit card or dull knife. If it is left in the skin it will continue to cause irritation. The bee is the only insect that will leave a stinger in the skin.

If the dog has been stung by one of the insects listed, administer a single strength OTC cold capsule. It cannot do any harm, and it contains an antihistamine that may stop an allergic reaction until veterinary help is obtained.

Stings and bites from certain arachnids, including the brown recluse and black widow spiders, scorpions, and tarantulas, are different. The pain is more intense and the wound heals more slowly, often with an open sore. The dog may have a generalized reaction accompanied by vomiting and shivering. The vomiting is probably a mild allergic reaction and the shivering is most likely due to generalized soreness. In any event, initial treatment is the same. Apply ice to the area and give the dog a single-strength cold capsule containing an antihistamine (if the dog is vomiting severely the cold capsule will probably not stay down). This generalized allergic reaction can lead to shock and death. Treat the victim for shock as directed later in this section and transport him immediately to the veterinarian.

POISONING

Dogs are curious creatures and like to investigate, which leads to many accidental poisonings. Often a dog will find an open can or bottle of some chemical and, accidentally or on purpose, spill it. The chemical gets on the dog's fur and paws, and in the process of licking the area clean, the dog swallows the substance. It is your responsibility as a pet

POISON EMERGENCIES

TYPE OF POISON	WARNING SIGNS*
Corrosive poisons Battery acid Corn and callous remover Dishwasher detergent Drain cleaner Grease remover Lye Oven cleaner	Burns on mouth Severe abdominal pain Vomiting Diarrhea Blood in urine Coma
Petroleum-based products Paint solvent Floor wax Dry cleaning solution Gasoline	Characteristic odor of petroleum Severe abdominal pain Vomiting Diarrhea Blood in urine Coma
Non-corrosive poisons Pesticides Fungicides Insecticides Lawn & garden weed killer Rodent poisons Snail & slug poison Antifreeze Ink Matches	Excessive drooling Vomiting Abdominal pain Lack of coordination

*In all cases of suspected poisoning, watch for signs of shock:
Pale or white gums, and rapid heartbeat and breathing.*

owner to keep all potentially toxic products tightly closed
and out of reach of your dog.

Poisoning symptoms are many and varied, as the
toxic substance can be swallowed, absorbed through the
skin, or inhaled. It's unlikely you will be on the scene when
the incident occurs, so it's important to recognize the signs
of possible poisoning listed in the chart above.

— HOW TO IDENTIFY AND TREAT THEM

TREATMENT

Do not induce vomiting.
Flush mouth and muzzle copiously with water.
Give one tablespoon of olive oil or egg white.
Take the dog and container of the suspected poison to the veterinarian
    immediately.

As above.

If dog has not vomited, induce vomiting immediately by giving one
    teaspoon of 3% hydrogen peroxide per 10 pounds of body weight
    every 10 minutes until the dog vomits.
If hydrogen peroxide is not available, place a heaping teaspoonful of
    table salt at the back of the dog's mouth every 10 minutes until he
    vomits.
Save vomited material.
Take the dog, the vomit, and the container of suspected poison to the
    veterinarian immediately.

Basic emergency treatment for different poisons is
as varied as the symptoms, so if at all possible, try to
determine the poisoning agent. This is important because
the first aid procedure that's appropriate for one type of
poisoning may be inappropriate or dangerous for another.
    For instance, if the poisoning agent is a corrosive or
a petroleum product, you want to control vomiting since the
returning chemical will cause further irritation and more
severe burns. In this case, give olive oil or egg whites in an
attempt to bind, or tie up, the chemical so it will not be
absorbed.

POISON EMERGENCIES (cont.)

TYPE OF POISON	WARNING SIGNS
Poisonous plants	Drooling Vomiting Diarrhea Abdominal pain Lack of coordination
Smoke or carbon monoxide inhalation	Depression Lack of coordination Heavy panting Deep red color to gums Possible convulsions

In all cases of suspected poisoning, watch for signs of shock: Pale or white gums, and rapid heartbeat and breathing.

However, if the chemical is not a corrosive or petroleum product, vomiting should be induced in order to empty the stomach of the poison. Of course, it is unlikely that you will see the poison being swallowed, so in either case professional help should be sought immediately. If the dog has vomited, the material should be taken with you to the veterinarian for analysis. He will also want you to bring the suspected poison container.

It is appropriate to mention here the existence of Poison Control Centers located all over the United States. If you ever have a poisoning emergency your local center, located through the telephone directory, can tell you the appropriate treatment and the proper antidote to give your dog until you can get him to the veterinarian.

In addition to the obvious poisoning agents, ornamental house plants can also be dangerous to a dog. It is safe to assume that all common house plants are toxic to some

---

TREATMENT

As above.

Note: If the dog goes into convulsions or has difficulty breathing, take the dog and a leaf of the suspected plant to the veterinarian immediately.

If conscious:

Remove the dog to fresh air immediately.

Flush the dog's eyes thoroughly by pouring diluted boric acid solution or plain water directly into them.

Transport the dog immediately to the veterinarian.

If unconscious:

If the heart is beating but the dog is not breathing, give artificial respiration by blowing into the dog's nostrils.

If the heart is not beating, begin CPR.

Transport the dog immediately to the veterinarian. Continue CPR on the way to the veterinarian or until the dog is breathing and the heart is beating without assistance.

---

degree, some more so than others. Dogs often like to chew on something green, so your best bet is to place the plants in areas where your dog cannot reach them and use hanging baskets for the more toxic types. If in doubt, call your veterinarian and tell him the type of plant you have or are going to purchase, and ask whether or not it poses a hazard.

Smoke inhalation is another possible threat to dogs. In the case of a fire, do not risk your own life to save your dog; leave that task to the firefighters or those trained in rescue.

If your dog has inhaled smoke, get him away from the area and into the fresh air. If he is conscious, flush the eyes with diluted boric acid solution or plain water to wash out soot and other particles.

If the animal is not breathing or if the heart is not beating, use artificial respiration and/or CPR. If the smoke is intense, the dog's airway and lungs may also be seriously damaged by inhalation of smoke and heated air. Burned lungs collect fluid, causing shortness of breath. To ease breathing, the dog's head should be kept higher than his body. Also, a burned airway may swell shut; it is imperative to keep this airway open, and immediate professional help is necessary.

Carbon monoxide poisoning can be caused by faulty heaters, but it is often due to carelessness. Dogs also often suffer carbon monoxide poisoning from being transported in car trunks—a dangerous and inhumane practice.

Characteristic signs of carbon monoxide poisoning are depression, lack of coordination, heavy panting, deep red gums, and possibly convulsions. Oxygen is needed immediately and the dog should be taken to a veterinarian at once. If there is no heartbeat or respiration, CPR is essential.

PUNCTURE WOUND

A puncture wound may be difficult to see because it is often covered with hair. If the wound is on the leg or foot, the first sign of trouble may be a limp. On other parts of the body you may notice slightly blood-tinged fur. The most common location for puncture wounds is the bottom of the paw, and these wounds frequently bleed heavily because the blood vessels are so close to the surface of the skin.

You can see the extent of the injury more clearly if you clip the hair around the area. Clean the wound with 3% hydrogen peroxide then examine it for an imbedded foreign object, such as a splinter or shard of glass, which you should remove if possible. Puncture wounds are deceptive; they can be deeper than they look and deep wounds often damage muscle tissue, causing fluid to accumulate. It is best to leave the wound open so that it can drain. This minimizes the risk of infection and swelling. A minor puncture wound that is kept clean should heal without veterinary attention.

An exception to leaving the wound open would be in the case of excessive bleeding or a chest wound. Chest wounds can be very serious. If the entire chest wall is punctured, a "sucking" noise will be heard as the dog breathes. The act of breathing causes outside air to rush into the chest and around the lungs, and lung collapse can follow.

Your first priority is to seal the hole in the chest quickly to keep air from entering. If a foreign object such as a stick or an arrow is in the chest, do not attempt to pull it out. This could open the hole further. Just bandage tightly around the object and take the dog to the veterinarian immediately.

SHOCK

Shock is a reaction to heavy internal or external bleeding or any serious injury that "scares" the body—for example, a large wound or amputation with heavy blood loss.

The body tries to compensate for the loss of blood by speeding up the heart rate to keep the blood pressure from falling. At the same time the blood vessels that supply the skin outside of the body narrow. This is to conserve blood so vital organs of the body can continue to receive their normal blood supply.

However, if there is heavy blood loss or other serious injury, the body overreacts and causes a pooling of blood in the internal organs. External blood pressure drops, and the supply of oxygen to the brain is reduced. If the brain is deprived of oxygen, brain damage and death result. Shock is a very serious condition and is the number one killer of dogs involved in accidents. It always requires professional care. Pale gums or cold extremities indicate shock.

When shock is present, your goal is to reverse the body's overreaction. Elevate the hindquarters to allow more blood to reach the brain. Stop visible bleeding to prevent a drop in blood pressure. Wrap the dog in a blanket with hot water bottles to help keep the body temperature up. (This is necessary because the external blood vessels become constricted and the outside of the body becomes very cold due to lack of normal blood flow. Raising the temperature of the outside of the body helps conserve heat). Then take the dog to the veterinarian as soon as possible.

UNCONSCIOUSNESS

If a dog is unconscious, check the vital signs immediately— is he breathing, and is the heart beating? If either sign is not present, clear the airway by removing any foreign material from the mouth and throat. Extend the neck so that it is not bent, and pull the dog's tongue so that it is hanging out of the mouth, and then start emergency treatment. If the heart is not beating, start cardiopulmonary resuscitation and con- tinue until the heartbeat is steady and the dog is breathing independently, or until you can get the animal to a veteri- narian. If necessary, have someone else drive you to the veterinarian's office so that you can continue to perform CPR on the journey. If the heart is beating but the dog is not breathing, begin artificial respiration.

In any case of unconsciousness, observe the dog closely for signs of shock. Shock greatly diminishes the blood supply to the external parts of the body and is indi- cated by paleness of the inside of the upper lip and the gums. Shock requires immediate treatment. It's a serious condition and when a dog is involved in an accident the animal is far more likely to die from shock than from its actual injuries.

VOMITING

Vomiting is nature's way of allowing the dog to rid the stomach of any substance—spoiled food, for example—that is, causing irritation. Vomiting is one of the problems most commonly encountered in veterinary medicine. Not all vomiting, however, is due to a simple cause; it can also be a sign of a viral infection or a disease of the liver, kidneys, or pancreas.

When a dog is vomiting, home treatment should be conservative. Food and water should be withheld for at least 12 hours. A preparation such as Pepto-Bismol can be beneficial because it coats the irritated lining of the stomach. You can give the Pepto-Bismol every four hours, at the rate of one teaspoonful or one tablet per 10 to 15 pounds of the dog's body weight.

After 12 hours, offer water, a little at a time. If the dog drinks too much, or too fast, he may vomit again. If the dog keeps the water down, offer a small amount of steamed or boiled ground beef, cooked rice, and cottage cheese. This combination is bland and easily digested. If the dog tolerates this food, you can make a gradual transition to a regular diet over a couple of days.

If the dog is still vomiting after 24 hours on this controlled diet, you must have a veterinarian check out the problem.

HOME HEALTH CARE AND FIRST AID SUPPLIES— A DOG-OWNER'S CHECKLIST

Rectal thermometer
Cotton-tipped swabs—for cleaning the ears
Mineral oil and eye dropper—for use at bath time
Dog nail clippers, slicker brush, and dog comb for grooming
Styptic powder—to stop bleeding from a nail
Boric acid eye wash
3 % hydrogen peroxide—this is a must for cleaning wounds
Antibacterial skin ointment—e.g. Bacitracin
Kaopectate for treatment of diarrhea
Pepto-Bismol for treatment of vomiting
Single strength cold tablets or capsules containing antihistamine—for treating allergic reactions or insect bites
Plastic or nylon eye dropper or dose syringe for giving liquid medication

Scissors

Tweezers

Adhesive tape, 1-inch and 2-inch rolls

Gauze bandage, 1-inch and 2-inch rolls

Sterile gauze pads, 3 x 3 inches and 4 x 4 inches

Towels

Triangular bandage and safety pins (for holding dressings in place

Blanket—for use in treatment for shock or as a stretcher

2-inch and 3-inch strips of clean cloth, 2-4 feet long—to tie an injured dog to a board stretcher or to make a muzzle

Wooden rule or tongue depressor for use with a tourniquet

Wooden paint mixing sticks and cotton batting for splints

Ice bags or chemical ice pack—for use in cases of heat prostration or burns

Empty distilled water or gallon milk containers for holding hot water

4-5 feet of 1/4-inch or 3/8-inch nylon rope for restraint

Note: Use medications *only* as directed in the appropriate sections of this chapter.